The Hockey News

EDITED BY EDWARD FRASER

TOP 10

Transcontinental Books

TO:

1. DKW
2. HCF
3. HJF
4. JAP
5. LF
6. PRP
7. RRH
8. SCF
9. SECF
10. THN

TABLE OF **CONTENTS**

TABLE OF **CONTENTS**

INTRODUCTION

We're an eclectic bunch here at The Hockey News.

We have 20-year veterans and we have rookies. We have Albertans and Britons. We have Olympic hopefuls and those who hope to one day learn to skate. We have pacifists and those who'd like to punch them for it. We have fans of the Flames and followers of the Panthers (and many teams in-between).

But there's one thing we all share: We love hockey…and we love to argue. And putting together this book gave us plenty of opportunity to partake of the latter. Most of the 65 chapters – a number we chose as a nod to our 65 years of publishing – were good for a verbal brouhaha as we hammered out the rankings. Voices were raised. Tables were pounded. Most importantly, however, we always came away smiling. And that's our hope as you pore over these lists. You may not agree, but we bet you'll flip the folio feeling informed and entertained.

There is plenty to digest over the following pages and in the spirit of the work here are the Top 10 Things To Watch Out For:

10. The (Not Always) Great One

Like all tomes that examine the pinnacle performers in hockey history, Wayne Gretzky's name is scattered throughout. He heads seven of our lists, including the one dedicated solely to his achievements. That's not surprising. What is, however, is the fact he doesn't take the No. 1 spot on five other top 10s.

9. The cost of war

We call hockey players heros for what they do on the ice, but there was a time when players chose to put their careers on hold to fight for their country. Now that's heroic. How did that decision impact their hockey legacy? We dedicate one chapter to those men, but the theme pops up in others, too.

8. A Hull of a player

Bobby Hull made an indelible impression wherever he played, as evidenced by his No. 1 stead on one NHL team's all-time top 10 and No. 2 spot on a second club.

7. Original Six…plus one

It's Hull's second stop that makes up the only team to get a countdown outside of the NHL's founding sextet. With all the excitement surrounding their return flight, how could we not reminisce?

6. Have a couple…

Two different Beers are served up. And one's imported.

5. Sweet 16

Nowadays, making an NHL team right out of the draft at age 18 is an impressive feat. One Boston Bruin, however, took on the world's best before he was 17 years old.

4. Sweet 51

Like Gretzky, Gordie Howe, who, incredibly, played – and played well – one year after his golden birthday, appears numerous times. His longevity is unmatched and his place in the game unquestioned...right? His stead among the Top 10 Red Wings caused the most fervent debate of any chapter and in the end was changed from its original position.

3. Who's that?

You surely know Gordie and Wayne and all the other legends, but what about Esa Keskinen, Vyacheslav Starshinov, Hod Stuart, Vladimir Martinec, Riikka Nieminen, Milan Chalupa, Vaclav Nedomansky, Dit Clapper, Rumun Ndur or even Wacey Rabbit? These 10 are drawn from 10 different chapters that'll add to your hockey knowledge...and vocabulary.

2. Oh how the game has changed

Ron Hextall – who takes a place on four forthcoming lists, including twice on one for skills with his gloves off – won the Vezina Trophy in his first NHL season, easily earning him a place among our Top 10 Rookie Goalies. But if Hextall put up the numbers he sported that season in 2011-12 he'd likely find himself in the ECHL: His 1986-87 save percentage would rank him 39th out of 45 NHL keepers, meaning 84 percent had a better save percentage this past season.

1. Young and old

The earliest birth date of a player listed is October 24, 1877; the most recent Sept. 6, 1993 – a span of nearly 116 years. And neither has played in the NHL. (Hints: The earliest is the only goalie among our Top 10 Pre-NHL Players. The most recent is the 'Grim Reaper' among the best Current Hockey Names.)

Enjoy the hunt...and the book.

Edward Fraser
Managing Editor
The Hockey News

GOALTENDERS

No matter how drastically the game changes, a great goaltender will always be a critical piece to a championship puzzle.

*Whether it's 1926 or 2012, NHL netminders have been relied upon as the last line of defense. From the days when dropping to the ice was prohibited, to the days where the stand-up style of play is almost extinct, goaltending has changed in many ways except for one: rarely does a team win a championship without a stellar star standing in the crease. This is THN's top 10 goalies of all-time. – **Bob Duff & THN Staff***

No. 3 | Martin Brodeur

10. Turk Broda, 1936-1952 – Toronto

It was late afternoon on the day of a Stanley Cup game at Maple Leaf Gardens and on the massage table in the Toronto dressing room, Maple Leafs goalie Walter 'Turk' Broda was partaking in his usual pre-game nap.

A few moments later, some of the minor leaguers called up as post-season insurance showed up and launched into a card game in the next room. Awakened by the noise, Broda politely suggested that they take their game elsewhere. When his request was rebuffed, the Toronto goalie took his pillow and smashed every light bulb in the room, leaving it in complete darkness, ending the card game and enabling Broda to resume his slumber.

These were the playoffs, after all, and when the big games were on the line, no one loomed larger between the pipes than Toronto's Fabulous Fat Man.

Broda, who died in 1972, was a solid performer during regular season play, a two-time NHL first team all-star and two-time Vezina Trophy winner. In the playoffs, Broda bricked up his net, lowering his goals-against average to 1.99 while winning five Stanley Cups and posting a then-record 13 shutouts. "Turk was the best playoff goalie of all-time," former Toronto teammate Harry Watson once said.

Only Jacques Plante (41) appeared in more Cup final games than Broda (38), who missed most of three seasons in his prime to serve in the Canadian military during the Second World War. Broda is the only goalie to lead his team from a 3-0 series deficit in the final when the Leafs beat Detroit in 1942.

9. George Hainsworth, 1926-37 – Toronto, Montreal

He stepped in for a legend and, later, stepped aside for another. In between, George Hainsworth fretted his way through a career dotted with records he still owns.

A 1917-18 Allan Cup winner with Kitchener, Hainsworth turned pro with the Saskatoon Crescents of the Western Canada League in 1923. After a 7-1 loss to Vancouver in his debut, Hainsworth's worrying ways came to the fore. "He wondered whether he made a mistake quitting the amateur ranks," former Saskatoon teammate Newsy Lalonde once told the Montreal *Gazette*.

Hainsworth was alone in worrying. "George's goaltending record with the Canadiens will never be equalled," Habs owner Leo Dandurand once said.

Dandurand brought Hainsworth to Montreal in August 1926 to replace legendary Georges Vezina, killed by tuberculosis earlier that year. Hainsworth won the Vezina Trophy, established in his predecessor's memory, the first three seasons it was awarded. In 1928-29, he posted 22 shutouts, limiting opposition shooters to 43 goals in 44 games for a 0.92 GAA, an NHL record that stands today.

So technically sound, Hainsworth, who died in 1950, made difficult saves appear routine, but felt the need to seek forgiveness for such excellence. "I'm sorry I can't put on a show like some of the other goaltenders," Hainsworth said in 1929. "I guess all I can do is stop pucks."

Traded to Toronto in 1933, Hainsworth gave way to Broda in 1936.

8. Bill Durnan, 1943-1950 – Montreal

Few careers were launched so remarkably. And even fewer ended with such suddenness. For seven shining seasons, Montreal goalie Bill Durnan put on a display of puckstopping that was unparalleled. Between 1943-50, he won six Vezina Trophies and was a six-time first team all-star. Then – amazingly, in the midst of the Stanley Cup playoffs – he announced he could do it no longer, walking away from the goal crease forever.

In between, Durnan won the hearts and minds of teammates and foes alike, and was hailed as the best goalie of his era. "My idea of a good goaltender is this type of guy," Canadiens teammate Murph Chamberlain told the Montreal *Gazette*. "It's the guy that doesn't bend under pressure that wins games for you and that's the type Durnan is."

Ambidextrous, Durnan could hold his stick with either glove, defying shooters to find his weak side. "He's so big, he doesn't leave you much to shoot at," New York Rangers coach Frank Boucher said in 1947.

Durnan set a rookie unbeaten streak record (12-0-2) and was unbeaten at home (22-0-3) in 1943-44. In 1948-49, he posted a shutout streak of 309:21. Less than a year later, at 34, he was gone, retiring during a 1950 semifinal with the Rangers, citing nerves. "He became gun shy," former teammate Elmer Lach recalled, noting Durnan, who died in 1972, had taken several shots to his face that season. "If there had been masks, he could have played a few more years."

7. Ken Dryden, 1971-1979 – Montreal

All he achieved during a nine-season NHL career was to win five Vezina Trophies, backstop the Montreal Canadiens to a half-dozen Stanley Cups, post an astonishing .743 winning percentage and earn induction into the Hall of Fame.

Yet Ken Dryden is often overlooked among the all-time great goaltenders, the prevailing sentiment being he was the product of the sensational team that played in front of him.

His Montreal teammates find this reasoning to be entirely without basis. "We had some great players, but if you look at what the team did the year he took off, you see what an important part of the team he was," former center Doug Jarvis told the Montreal *Gazette*. "They had the same players and they won when he was there and they didn't win without him. You need a goaltender who can make the big saves and Ken was that guy for us."

Clearly, Dryden travelled a different path than most hockey stars. He won the Conn Smythe Trophy as playoff MVP as a rookie with Montreal in 1970-71, leading the team to the Cup while simultaneously writing his exams at Montreal's McGill law school. In 1973-74, he sat out the season in a contract dispute, articling for his law degree.

He's found the arena of politics (he was a Member of Canada's Parliament from 2004 to 2011) to be a different world than the hockey rink. "When you win the Stanley Cup, your job is over," Dryden told the *Gazette*. "When you win an election, that's the start of the job."

6. Glenn Hall, 1952-1971 – Detroit, St. Louis

For a record 502 consecutive games, Glenn Hall guarded the Red Wings and Black Hawks nets without relief, but he's more often remembered for what he left behind prior to those contests.

It was his first Stanley Cup series, yet coach Scotty Bowman can recall that decisive Game 7 between his St. Louis Blues and the Philadelphia Flyers in the 1968 quarterfinal like it was yesterday. Things looked bleak when Hall, infamous for becoming violently ill before games, took Bowman aside, wearing a concerned look. "He told me that if he didn't have it, I should pull him out of the game early," Bowman said. "I'm just a young guy then, 33, and I'm starting to panic."

A short while later, Bowman noticed a pair of goal pads sticking out of one of the washroom stalls. "Hall was throwing up," Bowman said, "and whenever he did that, he always played a supreme game."

The first-year expansion Blues rode their goalie's queasy stomach to the Cup final. Even though Montreal swept them with four one-goal decisions, Hall won the Conn Smythe Trophy. "The scores flattered us," Bowman remembered. "We had great goaltending every game."

Called 'Mr. Goalie,' Hall won three Vezina Trophies and earned 11 NHL all-star team selections. He played in eight Cup finals and remains the only goalie to be a first team all-star with three teams (Detroit, Chicago, St. Louis).

5. Dominik Hasek, 1990-2008 – Chicago, Buffalo, Ottawa, Detroit

There are sacrifices we all make in our battle to outwit Father Time. Dominik Hasek is 47, but only two years ago he was still competing at a high level, spending a year with Spartak Moscow of the Kontinental League and posting an impressive 23-19-3 record with a 2.48 goals-against average and .915 save percentage.

Naturally, he paid a personal cost to maintain playing shape at an age when most goalies stop pucks only in their nightmares. "I am careful in my diet, but not completely strict," Hasek said at the time. "I still eat pizza and chicken wings once in a while, but I cannot eat the whole pizza like I used to, only one or two slices."

Hasek certainly had nothing to prove by extending his career. He would have been a surefire Hall of Famer had he retired in his mid-30s. His mantel was already full from his Olympic gold medal with the Czech Republic – the first time NHLers took part in the event (1998) – a pair of Hart Trophies and a half-dozen Vezina Trophies with Buffalo.

And then there are the two Stanley Cup seasons with Detroit, the second of which came as a 43-year-old. "I do not have any secrets," Hasek said of his longevity. "I just love hockey and treat it seriously. I know how to train and I work very hard."

4. Jacques Plante, 1952-1973 – Montreal, Rangers, St. Louis, Toronto, Boston

Plante's introduction of the facemask overshadows other innovations he brought to netminding. The six Stanley Cups he won with Montreal overshadow the record-setting achievements he garnered as an NHLer.

Plante's eccentricities overshadow the brilliance of his mind. "He studied goaltending with the methodical approach of a scientist," said Todd Denault, author of *Jacques Plante: The Man Who Changed the Face of Hockey*, the first biography of the netminder. "You can almost picture him, while the rest of his teammates were at the bar after the game, he's holed up in his room, making detailed notes."

After Plante retired in 1965, Bowman, coaching the Montreal Jr. Canadiens, lured Plante into making a comeback for an exhibition match against the Soviet Union.

Plante performed sensationally and the Jr. Habs won 2-1. He'd studied the Soviets' passing style so he knew where their shots would come from.

Donning the mask in 1959, Plante changed the look of goaltending. He was the first goalie to go behind the net to stop the puck. He'd bark instructions to teammates and roam from his crease to play the puck. Playing a position where mental state is essential, Plante's confidence never wavered.

Bowman planned to select Plante's rights from the Rangers in the 1968 intra-league draft, but Plante, out of the NHL for three years, but still ever the showman, had other ideas. "He came to the NHL meetings and called a press conference to announce his intention to return," Bowman said.

The Blues paired Plante with Hall – the two combined to earn Plante his record seventh Vezina Trophy.

3. Martin Brodeur, 1991-active – New Jersey

Martin Brodeur's career has turned into a Shakespearian play – Much Ado About Nothing. No one in history has put up as many zeroes as the New Jersey netminder, who ended 2011-12 with an NHL record 119 career shutouts.

He's also the NHL's career wins leader with 656. Those numbers have caused many to catapult Brodeur to the top of history's netminding heap. "I'm having a blast playing hockey," said Brodeur. "I know it's not going to last forever. I realize that. I want to cherish every moment of it."

As for the accolades, Brodeur will leave that to others, of whom there are many willing to step up and put their stamp of approval on the method in which he stops pucks. "He plays his greatest games in the biggest games," said Hall of Fame goalie Johnny Bower of Brodeur, a three-time Stanley Cup champion and four-time Vezina Trophy winner.

Breaking Terry Sawchuk's mark of 103 shutouts in 2009-10, Brodeur chalked it up to a process of the way the Devils play. "In our organization, for the longest time...they take a lot of pride in shutting down teams," Brodeur said.

In the era of the butterfly, Brodeur has achieved his milestones by playing a hybrid style that's more throwback than fall down. "You don't need to be a butterfly goalie to be a good goalie," Brodeur said. "When you have good mobility and you're able to skate really well, you don't need to go down on your knees all game long."

2. Patrick Roy, 1984-2003 – Montreal, Colorado

Bowman still thinks about December, 1995 when Detroit blew nine goals past Patrick Roy. Leaving the ice, Roy told president Ron Corey he was done in Montreal. "I remember thinking the next day, 'They're going to trade him. This could be bad,' " Bowman recalled. "And it was."

Roy went to the Colorado Avalanche and led them to a pair of Cups. "He didn't just stop the puck, he was our emotional leader," defenseman Adam Foote said. "He just wanted to win."

Roy stopped the traditional way of thinking about stopping the puck, making the butterfly style the chosen method for the elite netminder. "Roy created moves and changed the way goalies play," said former goalie John Davidson, the St. Louis Blues president in 2011-12.

Roy never put anything above the game's history and traditions. "My passion and respect for the game guided me," he said.

Such as March 26, 1997. Detroit beat Colorado, giving Mike Vernon his 300th victory. Roy slid the puck to Vernon, even though the two had fought earlier. "That was a classy move," Vernon said.

When he retired, Roy had won (551) and played (1,092) more NHL games than any other goalie, though Martin Brodeur has since passed both marks. During Stanley Cup play, his

No. 1 | Terry Sawchuk

151 wins and 247 games remain records. He won four Cups and earned a record three Conn Smythe Trophies.

Roy was an elite goaltender the day he arrived and was still considered one of the best the day he retired.

1. Terry Sawchuk, 1949-1970 – Boston, Toronto, Los Angeles, Detroit, Rangers

"He was the best." Jimmy Skinner, Sawchuk's coach with Detroit, said prior to his death in 2007.

Sawchuk is the only goalie in NHL history to post a goals-against average under 2.00 in each of his first five full seasons. An all-star on the ice, Sawchuk was plagued by injury and a lack of confidence. It was not uncommon for him to ask others whether he'd played well.

He set then-NHL records with 103 shutouts, 447 wins and 971 games played, yet feared he wasn't good enough to maintain his NHL position. Hall, who followed Sawchuk with the Red Wings, remembered sneaking into Olympia Stadium then situating himself to study Sawchuk's method of puckstopping. "I tried to copy his style, to use that low crouch which he played," Hall said.

Sawchuk was in goal for three Cup titles in Detroit between '52 and '55 and for the Maple Leafs the last time they won it in 1967. After being eliminated from the playoffs on April 29, 1970, Sawchuk got into a dispute in a bar. He sustained injuries and was hospitalized. Complications arose during his third operation and Sawchuk died of cardiac arrest. He was 40.

Hall bows in reverence to the man he watched as a teenager. "A lot of people think he was the greatest goalkeeper who ever played the game," Hall said. "And I include myself in that group." THN

WORLD JUNIOR
CHAMPIONSHIP SCORERS

The WJC is typically a reliable window to the future when it comes to showcasing the next batch of NHL superstars.

In this countdown we take a look at the deadliest all-time scorers from the annual battle royale for international junior hockey supremacy.

Each player featured in this top 10 would go on to a successful professional career, with only one of them never stepping foot on a NHL ice surface. **– John Grigg**

No. 10 | Eric Lindros

10. Eric Lindros, Canada, 31 points

The lone Canadian on our list, 'The Big E' was a man amongst boys as a junior. During three tournaments from 1990-92, Lindros tallied 12 goals and 19 assists in 21 games, helping Canada to two gold medals.

9. Esa Keskinen, Finland, 32 points

Keskinen never left Europe, but tore up both the Finnish and Swedish leagues after graduating from the junior ranks. He played 14 games during two WJC tournaments – 1984 and '85 – piling up 10 goals and 22 assists.

8. Niklas Sundstrom, Sweden, 33 points

The first of three Swedes to appear on the list, Sundstrom played in the 1993, '94 and '95 tournaments, scoring 18 goals and assisting on 15 others in just 21 games. The early '90s was the Golden Age for Swedish junior hockey; Sundstrom won two silvers and a bronze.

7. Markus Naslund, Sweden, 34 points

Naslund was a great junior, racking up 21 goals and 13 assists in just 14 WJC games in 1992 and '93, winning silver twice. In '93, he scored 13 times to set the record for goals scored during a single tournament.

6. Vladimir Ruzicka, Czechoslovakia, 34 points

Formerly the coach-GM of the Czech Republic's national team, but from 1981 to '83 he was one of the greatest junior players on the planet. Ruzicka gets the nod over Naslund for sixth place here because of his gaudy WJC goal total, 25 in 19 games. Although a triggerman, he tossed nine assists into the mix as well.

5. Esa Tikkanen, Finland, 35 points

Known as a two-way pest in the NHL, Tikkanen was a great junior player. He played three tournaments from 1983 to '85, teaming with Keskinen for the final two to form one of the more dynamic duos in WJC history. Tikkanen scored 17 goals and 18 assists in 21 games and helped the Finns to a silver medal in '84.

4. Alex Mogilny, USSR, 35 points

The first Soviet skater to make the list was a dazzling under-20 player from 1987 to '89. Mogilny scored 19 goals and added 16 helpers in 20 games. He was part of silver and gold medal-winning teams, but also took part in the 'Punch Up in Piestany,' a bench-clearing brawl in '87 that led to Canada and the USSR being disqualified from the tournament.

3. Pavel Bure, USSR, 39 points

The Russian Rocket made international headlines as a junior. He scored a WJC record 27 goals in 21 games from 1989 to '91 and added 12 assists to boot. In '89, Bure was the youngster on what many consider the best line in WJC history with Mogilny on the opposite wing and Sergei Fedorov centering. Bure won a gold and two silvers.

2. Robert Reichel, Czechoslovakia, 40 points

Canadians know Reichel as an Olympic-shootout heartbreaker, but many forget how dominant he was as a junior player. In 21 games from 1988 to '90, Reichel tallied 18 goals and 22 helpers, leading Czechoslovakia to two bronze medals.

1. Peter Forsberg, Sweden, 42 points

The most prolific scorer in WJC history did it all in just 14 games played from 1992 to '93. But it was the latter of those two tournaments that became Forsberg's coming-out party. Playing on a line with snipers Naslund and Sundstrom, 'Foppa' set records for most points in a single tournament with 31 (Naslund is No. 2 all-time with 24 in '93) and assists in one WJC with 24, 10 more than No. 2 Keskinen in '85. Forsberg's 32 career WJC assists are also a record. THN

No. 1 | Peter Forsberg

SINGLE-SEASON
PLAYOFF SCORING LEADERS

Garnering over 30 points in the playoffs is a big accomplishment. When you are only playing a maximum of 28 games, you have to notch better than a point per game to even think about hitting that mark.

To avoid repetition on this list – we're looking at you again, Mr. Gretzky and your high-flying Oilers – here are the 10 best point-leading totals from playoff seasons in history, with the caveat individuals can only appear once. **– JG**

No. 6 | Brian Leetch

10. Bryan Trottier, Islanders, 29 points, 1980

Trottier also led the playoffs with 29 points in 1982, but notched half as many goals as the 12 he had in 1980, the year the Islanders won their first of four Cups in a row and Trottier won his only Conn Smythe.

9. Danny Briere, Philadelphia, 30 points, 2010

Even though the Flyers didn't win the Cup in 2010, Briere was monumental in their journey to the final. The Flyers began the playoffs seeded seventh and worked their way to the top. Among his 12 goals were four game-winners.

8. Craig Simpson, Edmonton, 31 points, 1990

En route to winning the Oilers' fifth (and final) Cup in seven years, Simpson tied Mark Messier in total points, though he scored seven more goals. But neither skater won the Conn Smythe; it went to Edmonton goalie Bill Ranford.

7. Al MacInnis, Calgary, 31 points, 1989

The first of two defensemen on the list, MacInnis led the Flames in scoring by seven points and the playoff race by six on his way to a Conn Smythe Trophy. Calgary beat Montreal in six games for its lone Cup in franchise history on the back of the MVP's four game-winning goals.

6. Brian Leetch, Rangers, 34 points, 1994

Although not the highest scoring defenseman in a single post-season (that mark goes to Paul Coffey's 37 in 1985), Leetch led the league in assists and tied teammate Messier with four game-winners. That year the Blueshirts won their first Cup in 54 years and Leetch took home the MVP trophy.

5. Joe Sakic, Colorado, 34 points, 1996

Sakic led the league in goals and game-winners (six) as the Avalanche won their first of two Cups in six years. Colorado swept Florida in the Cup final; Dave Lowry led the Panthers in scoring with exactly half of Sakic's 34-point total.

4. Mike Bossy, Islanders, 35 points, 1981

The man with the highest regular season goals-per-game average (.762) amongst players with 200-plus goals in history was good for nearly a goal and two points per game in the '81 post-season. He led the playoffs in goals, assists and power play goals, but somehow lost out on MVP honors to teammate Butch Goring. Not to worry, Bossy collected the hardware in 1982, when the Islanders won their third Cup in succession.

3. Evgeni Malkin, Pittsburgh, 36 points, 2009

After staking his claim to the Art Ross Trophy in the regular season, Malkin continued his offensive dominance during the playoffs. With 36 points in 24 games, 'Geno' led the Penguins to a Stanley Cup victory over the defending champion Detroit Red Wings and proved that Sidney Crosby isn't the only superstar sporting black and gold.

2. Mario Lemieux, Pittsburgh, 44 points, 1991

Lemieux was simply magical in leading the high-octane Pens to their first Cup, beating the upstart Minnesota North Stars (15th overall) in six games; the Pens, for their part, finished the regular season seventh overall. Lemieux led the playoffs in scoring by 10 points over teammate Mark Recchi, recording the second-highest playoff point total in NHL history.

1. Wayne Gretzky, Edmonton, 47 points, 1985

Gretzky's 2.6 points-per-game average (47 in 18 games) will very likely never be matched. For leading the scoring race by 10 points over teammate Paul Coffey, The Great One captured the first of his two Conn Smythe Trophies. Gretzky had already led the post-season points parade the prior two years and went on to do it a total of six times, a record matched, appropriately enough, by just one other NHL legend: Gordie Howe. THN

No. 1 | Wayne Gretzky

LARGEST CONTRACTS

Chew on this for a second. Martin Brodeur's contract called for him to make $140,000 in 1994-95, a figure that was reduced to $81,200 thanks to a lockout-shortened season. That was the cost of a Cup-winning goalie less than 20 years ago.

The fast-forward button seems to be stuck on the NHL's financial landscape, as teams dish out big cash to get high-end, or at least highly paid, talent in their midst.

*Let's marvel at the Top 10 biggest contracts (in terms of total dollars) in NHL history. (We closed up shop on this list before the 2012 silly season, so don't be surprised at all if Zach Parise and/or Ryan Suter are now members of this club.) – **Kyle Palantzas***

No. 9 | Rick DiPietro

10. Nicklas Backstrom, Washington – $67 million

Despite an abrupt exit in the 2010 playoffs, the Caps reacted quickly in locking down the explosive pivot. The Swedish youngster signed a 10-year, $67-million pact during that summer, keeping the ever-so-dangerous connection of Backstrom-to-Ovechkin together for at least another decade.

9. Rick DiPietro, Islanders – $67.5 million

The oft-injured Isles goalie was the first player to sign a gargantuan contract coming out of the lockout. The 2000 first overall draft pick is cashing in $67.5 million over 15 years, but has played a mere 47 games the past four seasons. This, folks, is a prime example of a foolhardy contract.

8. Mike Richards, Philadelphia – $69 million

Richards captained just the third team in league history to overcome a 3-0 playoff series deficit, when his Flyers topped the Bruins en route a 2010 Stanley Cup final appearance. Richards came up short in that run, but got the job done in L.A. after Philadelphia shipped him and his $5.75 million cap hit to the Kings, where he won the Cup in 2012.

7. Duncan Keith, Chicago – $72 million

Behind his gold medal, Norris Trophy and Stanley Cup, Keith is hauling in the big bucks. The smooth-skating defenseman works hard for his money, placing runner-up in minutes played in 2011-12. The Blackhawks blueline investment is costing them $72 million over 13 years, making Keith the highest paid defenseman in history.

6. Henrik Zetterberg, Detroit – $73 million

The $73 million contract was enough dough to keep Zetterberg locked down in Hockeytown for 12 seasons. The 2008 Conn Smythe Trophy winner looks like he could be a Wing for life, just like his predecessor, Steve Yzerman.

5. Jaromir Jagr, Washington – $77 million

Jagr inked a seven-year, $77-million contract with the Caps in 2001, the largest deal at the time. The Czech winger, who signed before the salary cap days, earned more money per game than Bobby Orr made in three seasons.

4. Vincent Lecavalier, Tampa Bay – $85 million

Tampa Bay anchored Lecavalier to an 11-year, $85-million pact, keeping him, in theory, in the Sunshine State until he's 39. The deal makes Vinny the richest North American player of all-time, which is a touch cringe-worth considering Tampa's captain has averaged only 60 points over the past four seasons.

3. Alexei Yashin, Islanders – $87.5 million

Despite playing in Russia since 2007-08, Yashin is still being paid by the Islanders. New York bought-out his 10-year, $87.5-million deal in 2007, but the former NHLer will collect two-thirds of his original yearly stipend through 2014-15.

2. Ilya Kovalchuk, New Jersey – $100 million

In the summer of 2010 Kovalchuk signed on with the Devils for 15 years and $100 million in the summer of 2010. Despite the monstrous contract, New Jersey actually tried to sign the sublimely talented Russian to an even larger deal: $102 million over 17 years. The NHL rejected the contract, saying it was an attempt to circumvent the collective bargaining agreement, and fined New Jersey $3 million as well as a first and third round draft choice.

1. Alex Ovechkin, Washington – $124 million

The dynamic superstar follows Russian suit to the top of the list. The Caps captain signed a colossal 13-year, $124-million contract that made him Washington property for three more presidential elections. Since Ovechkin joined the Caps in 2005, the team's attendance has increased by more than 20 percent. It's a small – or at the very least, acceptable – tab to pay for a player who revitalized an entire hockey market. THN

No. 1 | Alex Ovechkin

INTERMISSIONS

For some, the notion of "best intermission" is where the bathroom lines are short and the beer lines are even shorter. That's what the 15-minute break between periods essentially provides: a chance for fans to grab a drink, relieve themselves and stretch their legs before settling in for more hockey action.

Of course, not everyone leaves his or her seat. The reason for that – at least in some NHL arenas – is because you might miss something more entertaining than the actual game. At its worst, an intermission means T-shirt guns and kiss cams. At its best, like in Nashville, it's practically a mini-concert. – Michael Traikos

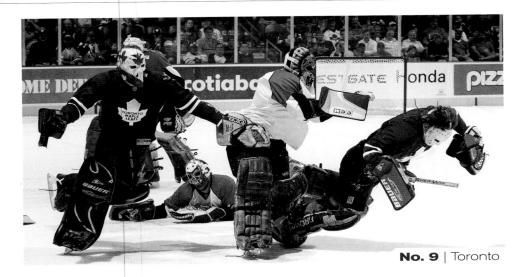

No. 9 | Toronto

10. Ottawa

The most shocking thing about an on-ice marriage proposal during intermission at an Ottawa game last season was not that it was between two women, but that it was a Senators fan popping the question to a Leafs fan.

9. Toronto

Game operations staff strap on the pads and transform the rink into a roller derby for the Great Goalie Race. A word of advice: never bet against 'Handsome' Johnny Luckowich.

8. Los Angeles

With celebrity-fans ranging from '80s sitcom stars like Alyssa Milano and Alan Thicke to uber-athletes like David Beckham and Wayne Gretzky, the Kings put on a show without even really trying.

7. Carolina
Cheerleaders and a chance to ride the John Deere-sponsored Zamboni are just two reasons why some teams can learn a thing or two from the so-called non-traditional markets.

6. San Jose
Lawnmower races are just as silly – and strangely entertaining – as they sound.

5. Vancouver
Usually, the million-dollar shootouts are letdowns. But in 2008, Prince Albert's Darwin Head successfully fired 15 of 20 pucks into the net from the far blueline to win four cars, a hug from Bobby Orr and a load of cash.

4. Tampa Bay
Two words: Lightning machine.

3. Buffalo
Hockey mascots are far more stationary than their baseball or basketball counterparts, but Sabretooth might be the exception. Not only does he play guitar and drums, he also rappels from the rafters like a paratrooper.

No. 1 | Nashville

2. Montreal
Former Expos mascot Youppi and steamed hot dogs make the Bell Centre a can't-miss for fans. But sometimes it is the players that get most of the action. Though it happened in Boston's TD Garden, Canadiens forward Mike Cammalleri was still stunned on Jan. 12, 2012 when he went to the dressing room after two periods and was told that he had just been traded to Calgary.

1. Nashville
Whether it's country legend Charlie Daniels fiddling around between periods or cheerleaders performing a line dance of high-leg kicks, Music City sure knows how to put on a show.

NON-NHL LOGOS

The NHL is filled with iconic logos, from the Original Six to the Flyers and Flames. But good design doesn't end there and it's only fair to shine some light on the other excellent crests in the hockey world. Here's our look at the best from across minor pro, major junior and Europe. The NCAA was excluded because its logos are almost always used for multiple sports. **– Ryan Kennedy**

10. HC Ocelari Trinec (Czech Extraliga)

Europe and dragons just seem like a perfect match and it's surprising more teams don't enter the fray, but maybe it's because Ocelari has the mascot locked down with its fierce visage. Trinec has been around since 1929, too, so they're no flash in the pan.

9. Lulea HF (Swedish Elitserien)

There are many, many polar bears out there, so how do you stand out from the rest? Forget about handing him a stick, just tell him to open those intimidating jaws as wide as possible and show off those fangs. For extra measure, Lulea includes some slashing colors behind their ursine mascot.

8. Seattle Thunderbirds (Western League)

Drawing off the iconography of local native tribes, the T-Birds bring one of the most unique logos out there in an excellent green-and-navy color scheme. The mascot is beautifully designed and harkens back to the days of the old pro Seattle Totems.

7. Barys Astana (Kontinental League)

The Kazakhs of the KHL have a nice snow leopard mascot as their logo, but the unique local lettering and color scheme really put this crest over the top.

6. Allen Americans (Central League)

If you're from Texas, you should probably have a five-point star in your logo somewhere and the Americans do it in style. Their razor-sharp 'A' is pointed enough to get the celestial design element in, but does so in a unique and subtle manner.

5. HC Lev Poprad (Kontinental League)

The Slovakian squad gives its Russian peers all they can handle in the visual department with a majestic lion set on a shielded crest. Nice colors and the addition of the lettering is classy.

4. Rimouski Oceanic (Quebec League)

It helps when Sidney Crosby and Brad Richards have donned your sweater, but Rimouski's logo is as good as they come in the Quebec League. Is it a ship? Is it a shark? It's both! And it's crashing through the water in search of a victim.

3. Florida Everblades (ECHL)

If you're a southern hockey team, embrace it. The Everblades come strong with their swamp-inspired pun name, then up the ante with a great-looking gator who goes that extra step, with skate laces crossing his snout.

2. Medicine Hat Tigers (Western League)

There are many tigers out there, but none can touch the WHL's vanguard. Sure, the white tiger of Liberec in the Czech Extraliga comes close, but Medicine Hat's vibrant, detailed cat rules them all.

1. Milwaukee Admirals (American League)

The Ads had an old classic cartoon mascot with his hat covering his eyes, but the new venture is bold and brash. The skeleton rocks a bone anchor on his cap and is impossible to miss in black and ice blue.

CURRENT
HOCKEY NAMES

THN caught March Madness fever in 2012, so we decided to create our own tournament pitting the best names in hockey against one another. We researched rosters from all major North American and European leagues to come up with a list of 64 active players. We then ranked them, split them into brackets and opened the polls to you, the readers, to decide who has the best name in hockey today. Here are the results, with the tournament winner at No. 1, the runner-up at No. 2, the semi-final losers at No. 3 and 4 (ranked based on our preference) and so on. **– Rory Boylen**

No. 10 | Cole Gunner

10. Cole Gunner

Is there a better name for a member of the Air Force Academy hockey team? The 21-year-old just finished his freshman year after spending three seasons in the United States League with the Fargo Force, Chicago Steel and Tri-City Storm.

9. Chase Golightly

The 20-year-old Temecula, Calif., native has spent two seasons with the Prince George Spruce Kings of the British Columbia League and last season logged 43 points in 58 games from the blueline.

8. Colton Yellow Horn

The 5-foot-6 winger was always better than a point-per-game player in junior and led the Western League with 48 goals as an overager. Undrafted, he has spent the past three seasons with the Central League's Allen Americans and led his team in scoring in 2010-11.

No. 1 | Kane Lafranchise

7. Tore Vikingstad

The oldest player on this list, 36-year-old Vikingstad made a name for himself with Norway at the Olympics by registering a hat trick against Switzerland. After spending a decade in the German League, he returned to the Stavanger Oilers in the Norwegian League last year.

6. Kale Kerbashian

The undrafted 22-year-old played for three different Ontario League teams and got a tryout plus four games with the AHL's Connecticut Whale in 2011-12. After that cup of coffee, he spent the rest of the season with the ECHL's Greenville Road Warriors.

5. Otto Honkaheimo

A long-time defender for Finland's Lukko Rauma (where Glenn Anderson and Dwayne Roloson played the past two lockouts), 'The Honk' was never drafted, but he has led his team in PIM for the past two years. He broke out with 27 points in 55 games in 2011-12.

4. Miles Death

Though his last name is actually pronounced "Deeth," Miles' name still looks cool. Death, 19, just finished his Grade 12-year as a defenseman for Minnesota's Wayzata Trojans. He's also a golfer – just as a hockey player should be.

3. Godric Tham

Tham, a 6-foot-2, 190-pound undrafted 20-year-old, played out of the Saskatchewan Junior League, where he was traded from the Melville Millionaires, Ron Hextall's junior team, to the Melfort Mustangs last season.

2. Wacey Rabbit

The most active contestant in social media, Rabbit took to his Twitter account to lobby for voting support. The former Saskatoon Blade was a fifth round pick (154th overall) of Boston's in 2005 and won a Memorial Cup with the Vancouver Giants in 2007. Rabbit lined up with the San Antonio Rampage of the American League in 2011-12.

1. Kane Lafranchise

The 24-year-old, and winner of our event, is working towards becoming the franchise player in the state of Alaska. An Edmonton native, Lafranchise manned the blueline for three years at the University of Alaska-Anchorage and spent the past two doing the same for the ECHL's Alaska Aces.

CONSECUTIVE
GAMES PLAYED

The modern-day NHL is as brutal and punishing as the league has ever been and players have a tough time staying in the lineup for an entire 82-game regular season, let alone building any kind of ironman streak.

But there are a select few NHLers who've demonstrated incredible durability over the course of not just one or two years, but for more than a decade. Here are the players who have had the longest consecutive games-played streaks – ***Adam Proteau***

No. 6 | Jay Bouwmeester

10. Mark Recchi, 570

The three-time Stanley Cup winner and 22-year-veteran played an incredible stretch of hockey for Philadelphia and Montreal from 1991-98. In one sense, each game of the streak mattered: when Recchi retired in 2011, he'd finished fourth in NHL history with 1,652 career games played – one more than Chris Chelios.

9. Billy Harris, 576

Harris played the first 576 games in the history of the New York Islanders franchise. The final game of his streak, which took place Nov. 28, 1979, was notable for an unrelated reason: it was the night Billy Smith became the first goalie to be credited with scoring a goal.

8. Johnny Wilson, 580

Wilson's consecutive games streak began with him playing in Detroit in the 1951-52 season and would extend until it spanned eight seasons and two changes of uniform when he was traded to Chicago, back to Detroit and then Toronto. The streak ended not because of injury, but a contract dispute with Leafs management.

7. Henrik Sedin, 581

The Canucks center and playmaking half of the Sedin twins nearly had his streak stopped in February, 2012 when he blocked a slapshot with his foot, but fought through it, showing the toughness that helped him set a new Vancouver team record (breaking Brendan Morrison's mark of 534 straight games) the same season.

6. Jay Bouwmeester, 588

The Flames D-man has displayed durability in his streak, which was still active at the start of the 2012-13 season. He also owns a less-positive-and-still-active streak: he's played 717 career regular-season games without making the playoffs. Ugh.

5. Andy Hebenton, 630

Known as 'Spuds,' Hebenton played more than a quarter-century of pro hockey and held the NHL record for consecutive games played for 12 years until Garry Unger broke it. However, if you count the consecutive games streak he put together in the Western League after he left the NHL, the Winnipeg native actually played 1,062 straight games until his father's funeral ended the run.

4. Craig Ramsay, 776

Ramsay won the Frank J. Selke Trophy as the NHL's top defensive forward in his final season as a player in 1984-85, but long before he had established himself as a stalwart who could always be counted on to be in Buffalo's lineup. His streak ended in 1983 after he broke a bone in his foot.

3. Steve Larmer, 884

Larmer's ironman streak started Oct. 6, 1982. For the next 10-and-a-half-years – all as a Chicago Blackhawk – the right winger was on the ice for every game until April 15, 1993. Sadly, he could have continued his consecutive games run even longer, but a contract dispute with Hawks brass forced him and the streak to the sidelines.

2. Garry Unger, 914

Unger's staggering streak lasted nearly 12 years (1968-79) and continued through his time with four NHL teams (Toronto, Detroit, St. Louis and Atlanta). It came to a screeching halt when Flames coach Al MacNeil made him a healthy scratch, but by then, he'd crushed Hebenton's iron man mark by 284 games.

1. Doug Jarvis, 964

The Canadiens defensive center and four-time Cup-winner began playing NHL games on Oct. 8, 1975 and wouldn't miss another game for more than 12 calendar years, nearly to the day. On Oct. 10, 1987, he was a member of the Hartford Whalers – the same team with which he broke Unger's mark – and coach Jack Evans scratched him for a game against Boston. Unfortunately, the end of his streak also was the end of his NHL career, as he played his final 24 games as a pro in the American League. THN

No. 1 | Doug Jarvis

DEADLINE TRADES

NHL fans go bonkers over their teams' chances at improving for the stretch run or peddling their moveable assets into futures. Here are the top 10 best Trade Deadline swaps of all-time. **- JG**

No. 6 | Vincent Lecavalier

10. Los Angeles trades Butch Goring to the Islanders for Billy Harris and Dave Lewis – 1980

We begin where it all began, with the biggest deadline deal at the very first trade deadline. Islanders fans will still say Goring was the catalyst for four straight Stanley Cups.

9. Buffalo trades Brian Campbell and its seventh round pick (Drew Daniels) in the 2008 draft to San Jose for Steve Bernier and San Jose's first round pick in 2008 (Tyler Ennis) – 2008

Campbell, an unrestricted free agent who they were sure to lose that summer, was the most sought-after blueliner to be dealt that year, but still disappointed in the playoffs. The Sabres certainly got the best of this swap in hindsight, as Ennis is now a burgeoning star in Buffalo.

8. Chicago trades Chris Chelios to Detroit for Anders Eriksson and first round picks in 1999 (Steve McCarthy) and 2001 (Adam Munro) – 1999

Chelios went on to play 10 seasons in Detroit, winning two Stanley Cups to go along with his previous win in Montreal. Eriksson played parts of three seasons in Chicago, scoring just five goals in 97 games. McCarthy and Munro, meanwhile, never made an impact with the Hawks or anywhere else.

7. Toronto trades Larry Murphy to Detroit for future considerations – 1997

Basically booed out of Toronto, Murphy was given to Detroit and finished a Hall of Fame career with two Stanley Cups in four seasons.

6. Tampa Bay trades Bryan Marchment, David Shaw and a first round pick in 1998 (David Legwand) to San Jose for Andrei Nazarov and Florida's first round pick in 1998 (Vincent Lecavalier) – 1998

Wouldn't the Sharks love to have a do-over with this one? Despite his hefty price tag, Lecavalier has 12 straight 20-goal seasons and has cracked the 70-point mark on five occasions. If it's any consolation, the David Legwand pick – No. 2 overall – was flipped to Nashville for No. 3 (Brad Stuart) and No. 29 (Jonathan Cheechoo).

5. Buffalo trades Rick Martin to Los Angeles for L.A.'s third round pick in 1981 (Colin Chisholm) and first round pick in 1983 (Tom Barrasso) – 1981

Like No. 6, it's not so much about the players traded, but who the pick turned into. Barrasso won the Calder and Vezina awards with Buffalo three years later. Martin, a member of the famed 'French Connection' line who passed away in 2011 at age 59, played only four games for the Kings over two seasons.

4. Dallas trades Joe Nieuwendyk and Jamie Langenbrunner to New Jersey for Jason Arnott, Randy McKay and New Jersey's first round pick in 2002 (Daniel Paille) – 2002

In a rare deadline-day blockbuster, Dallas was looking to get younger during a non-playoff season. New Jersey disappointed, losing to Carolina in the first round – although Carolina did get to the Cup final – but Nieuwendyk and Langenbrunner would help the Devils win the Cup the following season. On the other side, Arnott had three, 20-goal seasons in Dallas before moving on to Nashville.

3. Atlanta trades Marian Hossa and Pascal Dupuis to Pittsburgh for Colby Armstrong, Erik Christensen, Angelo Esposito and Pittsburgh's first round pick in 2008 (Daultan Leveille) – 2008

The surprise deadline deal was also one of the biggest in history. Pittsburgh rode Hossa, with his 12 goals and 26 points in 20 games, all the way to the Cup final (where they lost to Detroit, the team Hossa would sign with as a UFA in the summer). As icing on the cake, Dupuis continues in Pittsburgh as a top-six winger.

2. Washington trades Mike Gartner and Larry Murphy to the Minnesota North Stars for Dino Ciccarelli and Bob Rouse – 1989

Not sure what the Caps were thinking with this one. Gartner went on to score 311 more NHL goals and Murphy 665 more points. Ciccarelli did tally 276 more NHL goals, but Rouse? C'mon!

1. Hartford trades Ron Francis, Grant Jennings and Ulf Samuelsson to Pittsburgh for John Cullen, Jeff Parker and Zarley Zalapski – 1991

Some of you younger readers might not remember all the names involved, but Pittsburgh won back-to-back Cups with Francis, who finished his career as the No. 4 all-time scorer as the second-line center behind Mario Lemieux. Samuelsson was also key for the Pens, terrorizing opposing forwards with borderline hits from his blueline position. Cullen, who was coming off a 32-goal sophomore season and had 31 before the trade, played one full season with the Whale (26 goals) before he was dealt to Toronto. THN

No. 1 | Ron Francis

GOALIE FIGHTS

Fights are common in pro hockey and the NHL is no exception. When players drop the gloves, fans rise to their feet, their eyes glued to the combatants as they cheer on their favorites. Much less common: seeing goaltenders get hot enough to involve themselves.

The rare time it does happens, watching two goalies scuffle and awkwardly throw punches beneath an abundance of protective padding, is quite the spectacle. Here are our favorites. **– Liz Bevan**

No. 4 | Dan Cloutier vs. Tommy Salo

10. Ray Emery (Ottawa) vs. Martin Biron (Buffalo)

On Feb. 22, 2007, Buffalo's Patrick Kaleta hopped the boards and went after Ottawa's Dany Heatley. The Sens and Sabres began talking smack and shoving. Adam Mair singled out Jason Spezza and things got out of control. Chris Phillips retaliated against Mair before goaltenders Emery and Biron met at center ice. The only reason this fight makes the cut: the maniacal look on Emery's face as he removed his trapper and mask. Emery took Biron down and didn't stop smiling the whole time.

9. Ron Hextall (Philadelphia) vs. Alain Chevrier (New Jersey)

It was Jan. 24, 1987 and at the end of regulation the scoreboard read 4-3 for the Devils. The Flyers weren't happy about it. Mix in the fact Philly's Kjell Samuelsson ended up on the

No. 1 | Ron Hextall vs. Felix Potvin

receiving end of Steve Richmond's fist and you have a recipe for a line brawl. The players were indistinguishable amidst the chaos save for the goalies, Hextall and Chevrier, zeroing in on each other. The ice, littered with sticks and gloves, resembled an abandoned battlefield.

8. Steve Shields (Buffalo) vs. Garth Snow (Philadelphia)

Near the end of the second period May 3, 1997, there was a scuffle in front of Snow's net and he facewashed Sabres enforcer Rob Ray. Shields left the Buffalo net and headed straight for Snow. As famed Sabres play-by-play man Rick Jeanneret put it, "Shields says, 'Oh no you don't, I want to get a little piece of this action.'"

7. Byron Dafoe (Boston) vs. Patrick Lalime (Ottawa)

On Jan. 17, 2002, Hal Gill scored to make it 5-1 Bruins. Simultaneously, Ottawa's Chris Neil took a run at Boston's Bill Guerin, sparking a melee before Lalime finally stepped in. Dafoe skated the length of the ice and turned Lalime into putty. After a lengthy knuckle-chucker, Mike Fisher pushed Boston's Nick Boynton into Lalime, knocking him down and ending the scrap.

6. Dan Cloutier (Tampa Bay) vs. Steve Passmore (Chicago)

The rivalry between Cloutier and Passmore began in the minors. But on March 3, 2000, they took their show to The Show. Cloutier invited Passmore to throw down and even though Cloutier (6-foot-1) significantly outsized Passmore (5-foot-9), the fight ended up a draw. After the refs had positioned themselves between the two goalies, however, Cloutier caught Passmore with an extra shot.

5. Glen Hanlon (Vancouver) vs. Phil Myre (Philadelphia)

This fight qualifies as a bench-clearer. On Feb. 22, 1980, Philly's Frank Bathe jumped onto the ice to protect teammate Bob Dailey. Bathe's move had a domino effect, with every player on each side hopping over the boards with the intention of drawing blood. Even the penalty boxes emptied to amp up the carnage. Hanlon, the Canucks' backup goalie, and Myre, the Flyers' starting netminder, traded punches. Hanlon destroyed Myre with uppercuts. Vancouver coach Pat Quinn was suspended three games and fined $1,000 for signalling his players to leave the penalty box.

4. Dan Cloutier (Rangers) vs. Tommy Salo (Islanders)

Cloutier's fight with Tommy Salo of the Islanders came April 4, 1998. P.J. Stock tangled with Mariusz Czerkawski, ripped his helmet and jersey off and in came Salo. When Salo joined, Cloutier couldn't resist barrelling into the brawl to defend Stock. Cloutier got Salo's jersey over his head and forced him to his knees, punching Salo's head before he ragdolled and Cloutier backed off. Hungry for more action, Cloutier taunted the Isles bench afterward.

3. Patrick Roy (Colorado) vs. Chris Osgood (Detroit)

The vicious rivalry between Colorado and Detroit began in the 1996 Western Conference final and on April 1, 1998, it came to a head – again. Avs tough guy Warren Rychel dropped his gloves and started after Bob Rouse. In a heartbeat, the ice was covered with blurs of maroon, navy, red and white. It didn't take long for Roy to join the fray. Osgood and Roy skated to center ice. After a bit of jawing, Roy approached his opponent, turning his hands into fists, and started grappling. Osgood got the first punch in. They went shot-for-shot before Roy landed several in a row and Osgood was on the ground.

2. Patrick Roy (Colorado) vs. Mike Vernon (Detroit)

Peter Forsberg of Colorado started it things off March 26, 1997 when he took a swing at Detroit's Igor Larionov, but this massive brawl was all about retribution for Claude Lemieux's hit from behind on Kris Draper in '96. Darren McCarty went ballistic on Lemieux. The goalies got involved, too. Roy entered the scuffle and eventually found Vernon and Brendan Shanahan teaming up on Adam Foote. Roy took Vernon's head, cupped it in his glove and started wailing on Vernon's face. The crowd went bananas at Joe Louis Arena.

1. Felix Potvin (Toronto) vs. Ron Hextall (Philadelphia)

Toronto visited Philly Nov. 10, 1996 and Potvin made the mistake of slashing Daniel Lacroix of Philadelphia. Hextall skated the length of the ice and started throwing uppercuts; Potvin countered with some solid shots of his own. Who came out on top? If you listen to Philadelphia announcers, Hextall won the fight. Ask the Toronto guys and you hear a different story. Regardless, Potvin vs. Hextall comes out as the winner of THN's top goalie tilts of all-time. THN

CURRENT NHLERS
WITH IRISH NAMES

The Irish have a long history of producing excellent hockey players west of the Atlantic. Kennedys, Fitz-somethings, O'Reillys, O'Donnells, O'Connells, O'-everythings. We've seen many sons of Ireland play in the NHL, a trend continuing today.

In honor of our friends from the Emerald Isle we offer you our top 10 NHLers with Irish names. – JG

No. 6 | Ryan O'Reilly

10. Tim Connolly

It'd be tough to describe *Ó Conghaile* as "fierce as a hound" or "valorous," but that's what his name means, so we'll go with it. After eight seasons in Buffalo, the 31-year-old just completed his first season with the Maple Leafs, playing 70 games and notching a disappointing 36 points.

9. Matt Cullen

Ó Cuillin, derived from a "holly tree," can branch out and play both center and wing. His 14 goals and 35 points were good for fifth on the Minnesota Wild and can play in all situations.

8. Jamie McGinn

A trade from San Jose to Colorado gave *Mag Fhinn* a serious boost in production as his points-per-game average jumped to 0.76 from 0.39 after the deadline deal. Do the Avs have yet another burgeoning young gun in their midst with the 24-year-old left winger?

7. Chris Kelly

Ó Ceallaigh posted his best season statistically in 2011-12. Kelly is a decidedly Irish last name – the second-most popular in Ireland according to one website – and means "bright-headed." No wonder, then, that Kelly has turned into an all-around player.

6. Ryan O'Reilly

Ó Raghallaigh was a revelation in Colorado – second-rounders aren't supposed to make the NHL in their draft years – and he's only getting better. The pivot had a breakout season in 2011-12 with 55 points (18 goals), tops on the team.

5. Ryan Callahan

The Blueshirts finished first in the Eastern Conference and *Ó Ceallagcháin* set career highs in goals (29) and points (54). *Ceallagcháin* means "strife" or "contention," so *Ó Ceallagcháin* is a descendant of strife or contention. A fitting title for the Rangers' bang-and-crash captain.

4. Bobby Ryan

Picked second after Sidney Crosby in 2005, Ryan, a left winger, has a surname meaning "king." It's too soon to declare him NHL royalty, but it's not a stretch to crown him for his consistency: *Ó Maoilriain* has four consecutive 30-plus goal seasons.

3. Cam Ward

The name Ward translates to *Mac an Bhaird* in Gaelic, which means "son of the bard." While it hasn't exactly been sweet poetry for the Hurricanes since they won the Cup in 2006 – they've made the playoffs just once – there's no doubt Ward is a top-notch goaltender. He has 30-plus wins in five of the past six seasons and only played 47 games the year he didn't hit 30.

2. Dan Boyle

Boyle may just have the most interesting name on our list. You can call the blueliner "Dan vain pledge," which is what *Ó Baoill* means. Strange in that the Sharks have been making vain pledges to fans about their playoff chances for years…not that it's any fault of Boyle's.

1. Patrick Kane

His last name means "battler" and there's no denying that's exactly what *Ó Catháin* is. The undersized star isn't afraid to use what he has at his disposal – his stick, elbows – to keep defenders at bay. Now if he can just keep his shirt on.

No. 1 | Patrick Kane

RUSSIANS WHO NEVER PLAYED IN THE NHL

When the NHL expanded from six to 12 teams for the 1967-68 season, almost every minor-leaguer was bidding for a shot at the big time. Yet expansion did not tap into the vast pool of European talent, especially in the Soviet Union.

The Soviet government's refusal to grant exit visas to its stars from that era prevented them from ever playing in the NHL. In fact, it wasn't until 1989 that Soviet players were allowed to leave.

The Soviet national team that won nine consecutive World Championship gold medals between 1963 and 1971 might have been the strongest of all time. NHL scouts scrutinized the players when the Soviet team toured North America and even drafted some stars with the hope one day the government would change its mind, as the Montreal Canadiens did when they selected legendary goalie Vladislav Tretiak in 1983 towards the end of his career.

As far back as 1964, the Soviets asked New York Rangers GM Muzz Patrick for some exhibition games, but it took eight years before Canada's best pros and the Soviet Union clashed in the 1972 Summit Series.

Here are the best 10 Russian players who never played in the NHL. **– Denis Gibbons**

10. Alexander Ragulin

If 10 World Championship and three Olympic (1964, 1968 and 1972) gold medals weren't enough to earn him recognition, consider he was the first Soviet defenseman who developed the skill of blocking shots. More than half a century ago, he sometimes was referred to as the national team's third goalie. Ragulin was strong as an ox, but rarely crossed the line of dirty play.

9. Vyacheslav Starshinov

With reinstated pro defenseman Carl Brewer in the lineup, Canada was hopeful of finally shutting down the Big Red Machine at the 1967 World Championship. But Starshinov, a hard-nosed center who planted himself in front of the net and battled opposing defensemen, was more than a match for Brewer.

8. Boris Mikhailov

Mikhailov's shining moment came in captaining the Soviet national team to victory over the NHL All-Stars in the 1979 Challenge Cup. The Moscow native played with a lot of emotion and was perhaps the best pure goal-scorer in Soviet League history, connecting for 428 goals. He was a two-time winner of the Soviet player of the year award.

No. 6 | Valery Vasiliev

7. Alexander Yakushev

When the hulking left winger scored seven goals in eight games against Team Canada in the 1972 Summit Series, Canadian fans were astounded to learn he wasn't even the best player in the Soviet League. Two years later Bobby Hull called him the best left winger of all time.

6. Valery Vasiliev

Vasiliev captained the Soviet team to victory in the 1981 Canada Cup. A hard hitter, he was feared by opponents but also generated offense with pinpoint breakout passes and had a powerful shot from the point. Extremely strong on his skates, Vasiliev was named best defenseman at the World Championship three times.

5. Alexander Maltsev

A diminutive but crafty puckhandler, Maltsev appeared in more international games (321) than any other Soviet player and scored 213 goals. His moves were totally unpredictable. He starred against Canada's best pros at the 1976 Canada Cup and was recognized as best forward at the World Championship on three occasions.

4. Vsevolod Bobrov

The first great Russian star, Bobrov captained both the national hockey and soccer teams of the Soviet Union in the 1950s. He was a daring attacker who played the individual-style Canadian game and could easily switch the stick from his left hand to his right while beating a defender.

3. Valery Kharlamov

After watching Kharlamov play, Toronto owner Harold Ballard said he would offer him $1 million to play for the Maple Leafs. Kharlamov, who stunned fans at the Montreal Forum with two brilliant goals in the first meeting between the Soviets and Team Canada in 1972, had three skating speeds and used quick dekes to beat defenders.

2. Vladislav Tretiak

At the age of just 20, Tretiak sparkled against NHL stars in the 1972 Summit Series. He was outstanding again when the Soviets embarrassed Canada 8-1 in the 1981 Canada Cup final and once shut out the Montreal Canadiens 5-0. He was named European player of the year three times.

1. Anatoly Firsov

Canadians didn't see Firsov, an expert at dropping the puck back to his skates then kicking it ahead to his stick, perform against top NHL players because he ended his national team career six months prior to the Summit Series. Among his many feats, he won three Olympic gold medals, most notably in 1968 when he led the Soviets to a perfect record and scored a tournament-leading 12 goals and 16 points. His unmatched work ethic, quick thinking and lightning speed made him the best Russian forward ever. THN

No. 1 | Anatoly Firsov

ROOKIE PLAYOFF
PERFORMANCES

Whether it is the lunchbucket veteran who scores clutch goals, the journeyman defender who blocks shots and shuts down the opponent or an unheralded rookie who comes out of the blue to carry his team, each playoff season produces unlikely heroes.

In this Top 10 we take a look at the latter on that list. From goalies to goal-scorers, here are the young show stoppers who impressed us the most. – AP

No. 10 | Pat Flatley

10. Pat Flatley, Islanders, 1984

A 20-year-old right winger, Flatley scored nine goals and 15 points in 21 playoff games in 1984 as the Isles made it all the way to the Cup final before losing to Wayne Gretzky and the Oilers.

9. Cam Ward, Hurricanes, 2006

Just 22 years old at the time, Ward tasted his first playoff action in 2006 when he replaced Canes starter Martin Gerber in Game 2 of the first round against the Canadiens. Ward never surrendered the role the rest of the way, winning 15 games (including two Game 7s) and claiming the Conn Smythe Trophy as Carolina won its first Stanley Cup.

8. Jeremy Roenick, Blackhawks, 1990

Although he had played in the 1989 playoffs, Roenick technically was still a rookie the following season. So when the young center led the Hawks to the conference final in 1990 with 11 playoff goals, Roenick put himself second behind Dino Ciccarelli (14) for the all-time rookie playoff goal-scoring record.

7. Don Maloney, Rangers, 1979

The current GM of the Coyotes made a huge playoff splash in 1979. The left winger led all players with 13 assists and set a rookie record (at the time) with 20 points in 18 games.

6. Ron Hextall, Flyers, 1987

Arguably the last great Flyers goalie, Hextall won 37 games for Philly as a rookie in 1986-87, then followed that up with 15 wins and a 2.77 GAA as the Flyers got to the seventh game of the Cup final before falling to Gretzky's Edmonton Oilers. Hextall won the Conn Smythe for his efforts.

5. Ville Leino, Flyers, 2010

Though Leino played seven playoff games with Detroit in 2009, he was also still considered a rookie in his second playoff season. The winger was a relatively old 26 when he suited up for Philadelphia in 2010, but made the most of it, setting a new league record for playoff rookie assists (14) and tying Ciccarelli's record for rookie playoff points (21) set in 1981.

4. Ken Dryden, Canadiens, 1971

Dryden had played just six NHL games before starting between the pipes for the Habs in the 1971 playoffs. He pushed the Canadiens past the defending Cup-champion Boston Bruins in the first round and posted a 12-8 record and 3.00 GAA en route to claiming the Conn Smythe Trophy and his first Cup.

3. Claude Lemieux, Canadiens, 1986

One of the more underrated playoff performers in NHL history, the right winger first showed his post-season chops as a 20-year-old in 1986, scoring 10 goals (including four game-winners) in 20 games and helping the Habs to another Cup.

2. Dino Ciccarelli, North Stars, 1981

The right winger was 21 and had only played 32 regular season games when the 1981 playoffs began. He then set a rookie record for post-season goals (14) and points (21) in 19 games for a North Stars team that lost the Cup final in five games to the Islanders.

1. Patrick Roy, Canadiens, 1986

The Canadiens goaltending legend was just 20 years old in 1986 when he powered the Habs to the Stanley Cup and won the Conn Smythe Trophy as playoff MVP thanks to 15 wins and a 1.93 goals-against average. THN

No. 1 | Patrick Roy

LEFT WINGERS

Today, when young fans think of some of the best left wingers to play the game, chances are their minds wander to the likes of Alex Ovechkin, Ilya Kovalchuk and Henrik Zetterberg.

While one of those names has already established himself within the THN's ranking of the top 10 greatest left wingers of all-time, this is our opportunity to educate new fans of the game on some of the greatest to ever lace up skates, eight of whom had left the ice by 1980. **– BD & THN**

10. Aurel Joliat, 1922-1938 – Montreal

Aurel Joliat went on to become one of the all-time greats, but in the immediate aftermath of the deal that brought him to Montreal, fans wished they could have given him back.

In 1922, Joliat was acquired from Saskatoon of the Western Canadian League for Newsy Lalonde, who, despite deteriorating skills, was a legend. "It would have been like if they had traded (Jean) Beliveau in 1971 to get Guy Lafleur," said historian and hockey writer Bob Duff in 2008. "Lalonde had been the greatest player in franchise history to that point and people were pretty resentful."

But Joliat quickly won over the *Bleu, Blanc et Rouge* faithful, scoring two of his 270 career goals in his debut.

Even at 5-foot-7 and 135 pounds, Joliat never shied from the game's physical aspects and would often confront much bigger players, leading to his nickname, 'Little Giant.' He also played through numerous injuries during his career, including a bad back, separated shoulders and broken ribs.

Beyond his feisty style and impressive knack for goals (he was third all-time when he retired), Joliat, who died in 1986 at the age of 84, was known for his signature cranial attire. The 1947 Hall of Fame inductee donned a wool black cap at all times, even when he played, in order to cover a bald spot he was self-conscious of.

Joliat, a three-time Cup-winner, formed a potent duo with Howie Morenz. "If it wasn't for Joliat," Morenz once told reporters, "you wouldn't be writing about me so much."

9. Cy Denneny, 1917-1929 – Ottawa, Boston

All right, so Cy Denneny wasn't the most photogenic of players – he looks like grandpa out for some Sunday shinny with a belly full of pot roast, wearing a shrunken cardigan – but, boy, could he ever skate, score goals and guide his team to titles.

The 'Cornwall Colt' was hockey's first superstar left winger. During 12 seasons in the NHL, Denneny won the scoring title once and was runner-up five times, third once and fourth once.

Denneny led Ottawa to four Stanley Cups in 11 seasons in the 1920s, then was traded to Boston and was player-coach for another Cup champion in 1929. It was those early years that were building ones for Denneny. "A rookie had it pretty tough in our day," Denneny said

No. 7 | Luc Robitaille

in a 1949 interview with The Hockey News (Denneny died in 1970). "With six-man teams, it meant you had to play the whole game opposite a real established star.

"I remember the first game against the Canadiens in Montreal. They had stars such as Didier Pitre, Jack Laviolette and Newsy Lalonde, so you can imagine how I felt that night."

Denneny did just fine those early years. His 36 goals in 20 games in 1917-18 were second only to Joe Malone's 44 tallies. His 333 points was a league high when he retired in 1929.

Denneny is also credited with being the first player to use a curved stick. "I always used a slightly hooked stick," he said, "and by a certain flick of the wrist I could get that puck to curve, hook or drop at a goalie."

8. Alex Ovechkin, 2005-active – Washington

Before the NHL closed its doors for 2004-05, the next superstar was drafted when Alex Ovechkin went first overall to the Washington Capitals.

While 'Ovie' would surely have stepped right into the NHL after being drafted, he had to wait until his 20-year-old season to shine. And with a new feel in the NHL game after the lockout, Ovechkin was able to thrive on his speed, strength and shot.

"When he skates, he's hard to stop," said Detroit's Pavel Datsyuk. "He's strong and has a good shot."

Ovechkin joined the league with another young star, Pittsburgh's Sidney Crosby, and the two were immediately pitted against one another. But it was Ovechkin who won the initial race, taking home the Calder Trophy with a 52-goal, 106-point season.

It didn't stop there. Nabbing nightly spots on highlight reels with outstanding goals, Ovechkin reached 50 tallies four times in five seasons. In 2007-08, Ovechkin became the first to win the Art Ross, Rocket Richard, Lester Pearson and Hart honors in the same year.

Ovechkin scored 65 goals during that award-packed season, setting a new record for a left winger. Through five seasons, Ovechkin was named a first-team all-star five times, becoming the first player to achieve that feat to kick off a career.

7. Luc Robitaille, 1986-2006 – Pittsburgh, Rangers, Detroit, Los Angeles

Luc Robitaille's career beautifully – and bountifully – demonstrated that you don't have to be fast to be quick.

From the time he was young, Robitaille heard the whispers he was just a little too lumbering on the left side to be a lethal goal-scorer. "I remember asking my dad when I was a kid, 'Dad, am I really slow?' and he said, 'Son, whenever there's a loose puck, you seem to be first on it,' " Robitaille recalled. "And then I took pride in that, to jump on loose pucks and always try to be first."

Between the bluelines, Robitaille was never going to overwhelm anybody. But bouncing between the corners and the front of the net was a different story, thanks largely to the fact 'Lucky Luc' worked tirelessly to gain an edge in that all-important space. "I worked on my quickness every day," he said. "If I was in front of the net and the puck was in the corner, I knew I had a good first three steps because I worked on it every day."

The effort produced 668 career goals from the port side, more than any left winger in the history of the game. Robitaille's preparation went beyond doing drills in practice. Especially in the early days of his career, his always smiling persona belied a mind that never stopped turning over aspects of the game he loved. "Even though I always seemed to be the happy guy," said Robitaille," personally, I was never happy with what I had done. I always wanted to do better."

6. Busher Jackson, 1929-1944 – Toronto, New York Americans, Boston

As the flashiest member of Toronto's vaunted 'Kid Line,' Harvey 'Busher' Jackson was a brash young man with a wicked backhand. Even his nickname was backhanded.

Legend has it he picked up the tag when he refused to carry sticks for the trainer while injured, a tradition at the time. The trainer branded him 'Busher' as in 'bush league' and the name stuck, even though Jackson's play was anything but.

Skating alongside Joe Primeau and Charlie Conacher, Jackson led the NHL in 1931-32 with 28 goals and 53 points. That year also saw him hoist his only Cup, as the Leafs knocked off the Rangers in a three-game sweep. Jackson's seven points led the squad.

After a decade in Toronto, Jackson was traded to the New York Americans, then to Boston two seasons later for cash. In his second-last season, he helped the Bruins to the 1943 Cup final, where they were swept by Detroit.

Jackson battled alcoholism and unemployment once his playing days were finished, tarnishing his name in the minds of many. In 1958, he fell down a flight of stairs, breaking his neck and prompting a lengthy stay in a Toronto hospital. He maintained at the time that it was simply bad luck. "People will say I was loaded," Jackson told THN at the time. "There have been times when it might have happened because I was stiff. This wasn't one of them."

Jackson died in 1966 at 55 and was inducted into the Hall of Fame in 1971.

5. Johnny Bucyk, 1955-1978 – Detroit, Boston

Johnny Bucyk was nicknamed 'Chief', but just as appropriately could have been called 'Rock.' At six-foot, 195 pounds, Bucyk had a large frame for his day and used it effectively, carving a reputation as a feared body-checker. He was also considered a clean player, as his two Lady Byngs attest.

At the same time, he was a solid and consistent point producer, occasionally bordering on spectacular, particularly towards the end of his career. The Edmonton native recorded 20-plus goals 16 times, punctuated by a 51-goal explosion in 1970-71 at age 35.

Playing with the likes of Phil Esposito and Bobby Orr in Boston didn't hurt, but Bucyk – still the Bruins franchise scoring king with 545 goals and second to Ray Bourque in points with 1,330 – merits credit for developing a knack of quietly getting open, usually just near a goal post, to bang home a loose puck or finish a nice feed. "The 'Chief' brought stability and was the most consistent player I ever played with or against," Esposito said. "He was always there. You didn't notice him much, but at the end of the night you look and he had a goal and three assists or two goals and an assist."

Bucyk was Boston's captain for five seasons, just before and after the club's two Stanley Cup runs in 1970 and '72. Despite not wearing a 'C' during the championship years, his teammates still looked up to him…if not for his leadership on the ice alone. "We all considered (him) our captain," Esposito said, "because he could arrange the best parties."

4. Dickie Moore, 1952-1968 – Montreal, Toronto, St. Louis

If you're a do-it-yourselfer and your drill dies, you can rent one from Dickie Moore. For bigger jobs you can pick up a 6,000-pound excavator – and everything in between. Nowadays you can find the six-time Stanley Cup winner at his desk, where he's president of Dickie Moore Rentals.

No. 1 | Bobby Hull

Moore could play the game any way – in the back alley, along the boards or dangling in the offensive zone – so it's no shock that he carved a post-career niche for himself. Just as was the case on the ice, nothing can stop him. A broken wrist couldn't keep him from winning the first of two scoring titles in 1958 and a host of injuries couldn't keep him from putting together a Hall of Fame career.

Moore is stubbornly true to his roots, which began in the working-class neighborhood of Park Extension in Montreal. Even after he cracked the Canadiens lineup, Moore worked summers in construction.

He jokes that he still has to make a living, but what drives him is that he doesn't know any other kind of life. "My work keeps me alive, keeps me pumping," Moore said. "And nobody can fire me. Why would I take it easy? Have you ever seen these retired guys? I just saw them the other day in the shopping center and their heads bob up and down. And they're bored."

Chances are that will never happen with Moore. It certainly never happened when he played. He was tough, rambunctious and drove the net like a demon.

3. Frank Mahovlich, 1956-1974 – Toronto, Detroit, Montreal

Every time he stepped on the ice, Frank Mahovlich left no doubt he was a Hall of Fame talent. It can be argued the toughest challenge the left winger ever fought was the off-ice battle to be understood.

In spite of leading Toronto to his first of six Stanley Cups in 1961-62, Mahovlich drew the wrath of then-Toronto GM Punch Imlach during a contract dispute. Mahovlich would hear boos even from the home crowd at Maple Leaf Gardens.

The pressure of playing 11-plus seasons with the Leafs took a toll on Mahovlich, who believed NHL players were underpaid. He suffered from depression more than once, but fought through it to play 22 years (18 in the NHL and four in the WHA) of professional hockey. "A very classy man and highly misunderstood," said Mark Napier, a teammate of Mahovlich with the Toros. "Frank is a real deep thinker; sometimes you'd ask him a question and you'd get an answer two days later. He was a little bit shy and could come off as a little standoffish.

"But I got to know him very well. He's got a good, dry sense of humor. I have a lot of respect for that man. I'm sure it couldn't have been easy to live a normal lifestyle back in Toronto in those days."

Mahovlich's critics couldn't deny him respect. He scored 30 or more goals nine times in the NHL and was the first NHLer ever to score 40 or more with three different franchises.

2. Ted Lindsay, 1944-1965 – Chicago, Detroit

His face is chiseled with the marks of more than 700 stitches received during his career from what he likes to call "amateur plastic surgery" performed by opponents.

Ted Lindsay knew one way to play and he makes no apologies for the style that earned him the tag 'Terrible Ted.' "I had the idea that I should beat up every player I tangled with and nothing ever convinced me it wasn't a good idea," Lindsay said. "You had to play tough in those days or they'd run you out of the building."

Lindsay led the NHL in goal-scoring with 33 in 1947-48 and won the Art Ross Trophy as NHL scoring leader with 78 points in 1949-50. He also won an NHL penalty-minute crown with Chicago in 1958-59 and retired as the league's career leader in PIM, making few friends along the way. "You'd get to the All-Star Game and Ted Lindsay would walk by and grunt," Andy Bathgate remembered. "That's the only words you'd get out of him."

Lindsay was part of four Stanley Cup winners with Detroit. In 1991, when Lindsay's No. 7 was retired by the Wings, the softer side of him surfaced: "If I had two wishes, one would be that my mother and father were here, because it was their upbringing which made it possible," he said, before casting his eyes toward a pair of skates presented to him as a gift. "My second wish would be that I could put on these skates and don that Red Wing uniform one more time."

1. Bobby Hull, 1957-1980 – Chicago, Winnipeg, Hartford

To Bobby Hull, the entertainment experience for those who frequented Chicago Stadium extended beyond what they saw him do with one of those bow-bladed sticks. "I felt they deserved a part of me when they came to see me play," he said. "We had a love affair and that's the way it went.

"My dad told me when I was very young: 'See that sheet of ice son? Every inch of it belongs to you,' " Hull said. "And I was going to use every inch of that ice. I knew I had to be the best on the ice every shift I was out there and the way to get people's eye was to get that biscuit and do something with it."

Talking about Hull and not addressing the curved blade would be like doing a 1-on-1 with Luke Skywalker and not asking about his lightsaber. According to Hull, the advancement came about because of Stan Mikita's spiteful nature towards the sticks the Hawks were supplied with. During one practice, Mikita tried to foul the lumber by sticking it in the door jamb of the bench. The two crafted more efficient ways to bend their blades and goalies were sent scrambling.

Hull's shot helped him become a five-time 50-goal scorer and set a new single-season mark in 1965-66 with 54 tallies, before breaking his own record with 58 in 1968-69. 🅣🅗🅝

FIGHTERS

There are fewer things more difficult as a hockey observer than comparing players from different eras, so you won't find any Eddie Shores or Sprague Cleghorns on this list. And we've only gone with guys who played for a number of years, so, sorry, Link Gaetz, despite you're 412 PIMs in 65 games, you're out.

And this isn't a straight PIMs list, it's is a concoction of antics and reputations...and we can't help love the guys who could chip in with some offense as well. – JG

No. 8 | Tie Domi

10. Stan Jonathan – Boston, Pittsburgh

A full-blooded native Canadian, Jonathan played during the Big, Bad Bruins era and was a fan favorite. In the late 1970s and early 1980s he was one of the NHL's most-feared fighters, but he had some hands, too, twice scoring 21 or more goals.

9. Terry O'Reilly – Boston

Oh those '70s and '80s Bruins. Those were the days between when every player had to be able to stand up for himself and when designated goons came into vogue. O'Reilly could play it rough-and-tumble or he could score. In 12 full seasons, he failed to score double-digit goals just twice and popped 20 or more four times. Oh, and he totalled nearly 2,100 PIMs during his career.

8. Tie Domi – Rangers, Winnipeg, Toronto

Domi sits third all-time in PIM with 3,515, a pretty amazing feat since he's listed at a generous 5-foot-10. The little fighter who could took on all comers and was one of the league's first modern sideshows. He topped-out at 365 PIMs in 1997-98 and never totalled fewer than 109 when playing a full season (he had 42 in 1989-90, but played just two games). He could do more than fight, but that's what he'll be remembered for.

7. Marty McSorley – Pittsburgh, Edmonton, Los Angeles, Rangers, San Jose, Boston

Fourth all-time in PIM, McSorley was Wayne Gretzky's protector in Los Angeles and could play some, too. A defenseman, he scored 20 or more points 10 times and was lauded for his leadership on and off the ice. His career came to an ignominious end with the Donald Brashear incident, but McSorley was no simple goon.

6. Dave Semenko – Edmonton, Toronto

Semenko was the arguably the toughest hombre of the 1980s, except he got to skate alongside The Great One in Edmonton, which is how he managed to score double-digit goals three times. He pioneered the designated bodyguard/goon position and did it as well as anyone.

5. Georges Laraque – Edmonton, Phoenix, Pittsburgh, Montreal

Laraque was the undisputed heavyweight champ of the league during his seven-plus seasons in Edmonton. He was so feared that often he couldn't find a partner to dance with. It's strange that this beast of a man who could eat his opponents alive is a vegan.

4. Dave Williams – Toronto, Vancouver, Detroit, Los Angeles, Hartford

The all-time PIM leader with 3,966, 'Tiger' was as entertaining as they come. He'd fight anyone who'd drop them and is famous for riding his stick cowboy style after scoring a goal, something he did 241 times during his career. His best season came with the Canucks in 1980-81: 35 goals, 62 points, 343 PIMs.

3. Dave Schultz – Philadelphia, Los Angeles, Pittsburgh, Buffalo

'The Hammer' won two Stanley Cups with the Flyers and was the poster boy for the Broad Street Bullies. No player comes within 63 PIM of Schultz's 472 in 1974-75. He scored 20 goals the season before, but dipped to nine during his record-setting campaign. His career PIM-per-game average is 4.3.

2. John Ferguson – Montreal

Ferguson is considered the NHL's original policeman, but he was so much more. During his eight NHL seasons he finished outside the top nine in PIM just once (he was 11th in 1967-68), won five Cups, scored 15 or more goals seven times and played with (and held his own with) some of the greatest players the game has known.

1. Bob Probert – Detroit, Chicago

Probert is fifth all-time with 3,300 PIM, but he was the most skilled of anyone on this list. Ferguson once said as good as he was at his role, he was no Probert. His best season came in 1987-88 with the Wings: 29 goals (including 15 power play markers and five game-winners), 62 points (he added another 21 points in 16 playoff contests), a plus-16 rating and 398 PIM. Heady numbers to be sure and worthy of the top spot. THN

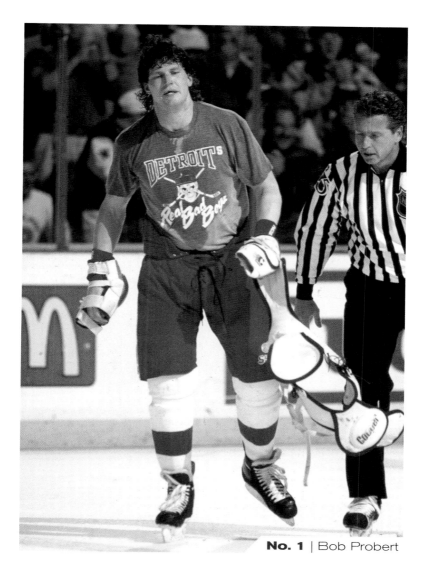

No. 1 | Bob Probert

DEADLY SHOTS

There's more than one way to score a goal in the NHL. Sometimes, it's an amazing individual effort, a beautiful passing play or even a mishap by the padded man. There are players who drive to the net and score through sheer force of will and others who pick their spots on the ice to uncork a deadly shot.

In this countdown we look at the masters of the latter category. **– Brian Liu**

No. 9 | Steven Stamkos

10. Bernie Geoffrion

'Boom-Boom' was one of the most prolific scorers of his era, becoming the second player, after Rocket Richard, to reach 50 goals in a season. A long-time Canadien, Geoffrion slapped his way to 393 goals in 16 NHL seasons – popularizing the big shot.

9. Steven Stamkos

It's still early in this Markham, Ont., native's career, but at only age 22 Stamkos has already won two Rocket Richard Trophies. There's no question he's the deadliest one-timer artist in the league and with Martin St-Louis feeding him pucks he should continue that trend for years to come.

8. Al Iafrate

This 6-foot-3, 240-pound bruiser quarterbacked NHL power plays for more than a decade. Drafted fourth overall in 1984 by the Maple Leafs, Iafrate was rushed to the NHL, but eventually developed into a consistent point producer with a rocket from the blueline. Iafrate scored 20 goals three times, but he was forced to retire at age 32 due to chronic knee injuries. He retired with the hardest shot in skills competition history (105.2 mph).

7. Joe Sakic

Sakic was the unquestioned master of the wrist shot during his time, with his quick wrister bettering the slapshots of most players in the league. The pride of Burnaby, B.C., scored 625 goals over his 20-year career, all with the Colorado organization. The sight of 'Super Joe' streaking down the wing and unleashing a blink-and-you'll-miss-it wrist shot past a frozen goalie is still an enduring image.

6. Zdeno Chara

Iafrate's record for the hardest shot stood for 16 years until Chara broke it with a 105.4 mph blast in 2009. Two years later, Chara would break his own record with a 105.9 mph shot and again a year later with 108.8. The Islanders drafted Chara for his 6-foot-9 frame, but it took four years and a trade to Ottawa before the big Slovak broke out. He doesn't score as much as you would think (his career-high in goals is 19), but shot-blockers are terrified.

5. Jari Kurri

Wayne Gretzky's triggerman during the Oilers dynasties of the '80s, Kurri was a dangerous one-timer specialist and one of the most money goal-scorers ever. The right winger had 106 playoff markers, including 14 game-winners, and he shares the record with Reggie Leach for most goals in a playoff run (19).

4. Bobby Hull

Along with fellow Black Hawk Stan Mikita, 'The Golden Jet' was one of the first players to use a curved stick. The puck leapt off the elder Hull's weapon – he still has the hardest slapshot ever recorded at 118.3 mph (though speed guns were less reliable back then). Hull would have finished with many more than 610 NHL goals had he not played seven years in the upstart WHA, where he scored another 303 markers.

3. Al MacInnis

MacInnis announced his presence to the league during his rookie season when he scored on Mike Liut of the St. Louis Blues. MacInnis skated in from the blueline and blasted a shot that cracked Liut's mask, knocked the goalie down and bounced into the net. MacInnis quickly developed a reputation for putting players on the disabled list: In 1999, he injured teammate and goalie Rich Parent during warmups, breaking his protective cup and rupturing a testicle.

2. Mike Bossy

Bossy retired at age 30 due to back problems, but the winger scored 573 goals and his .762 goals per game is still the highest mark in NHL history. Bryan Trottier passing to Bossy in the slot would result in a near automatic goal in the '80s. His insanely quick release was a nightmare for goalies. Bossy stands 20th on the all-time goals list.

1. Brett Hull

The 'Golden Brett' could score in a variety of ways, but the image of Hull, dropped down on one knee and stick raised in his follow-through is one of the most iconic in hockey history. He used that famed one-timer to score 86 goals in '90-91, third-most in a single season behind Gretzky. Only The Great One and Mr. Hockey have more than Hull's 741 career goals. ᴛʜɴ

No. 1 | Brett Hull

OVERTIMES

If there's one thing the Stanley Cup playoffs bring each year, it's drama. Upsets, seventh games, veterans striving for their first Cup and young players getting a taste of what it takes to win all make the post-season grind unique.

*And then, of course, there's overtime. Some of the greatest playoff games in NHL history have gone to an extra period…or six. Here are our most memorable overtimes. – **JG***

No. 8 | NY Islanders vs. Washington

10. Dallas 2, San Jose 1 – 2008 (9:03 of the fourth overtime period)

Brenden Morrow ended an exhausting conference semifinal that saw four of six games go to overtime. Morrow's power play goal came courtesy Sharks defenseman Brian Campbell, who put the puck over the glass from inside his blueline.

9. Philadelphia 2, Pittsburgh 1 – 2000 (12:01 of 5OT)

With fans sleeping in the stands, Keith Primeau ended the third-longest game in NHL history with his first career playoff goal. Primeau's marker tied the conference semifinal 2-2 and the Flyers took the series in six games.

8. Islanders 3, Washington 2 – 1987 (8:47 of 4OT)

Pat Lafontaine's seeing-eye slapper from the top of the faceoff circle ends the longest Game 7 in history. Islanders goalie Kelly Hrudey makes an incredible 73 saves in backstopping his team to a first round victory, while Caps netminder Bob Mason stops a "mere" 54 shots in the 'Easter Epic.'

7. Detroit 1, Montreal Maroons 0 – 1936 (16:30 of 6OT)

Mud Bruneteau nets the deciding marker in the longest game in NHL history with a tally that's remembered as the result of fatigue, rather than skill. Detroit goes on to defeat the Toronto Maple Leafs in the final. If they had TV then, this might be No. 1.

6. Detroit 4, Rangers 3 – 1950 (8:31 of 2OT)

Pete Babando scores the winner in the first Stanley Cup final Game 7 to go to overtime. Four years later, another Red Wing – Tony Leswick – gets the game-winner in the last Cup final series to go to overtime in Game 7.

5. Montreal 3, Calgary 2 – 1986 (0:09 of OT)

In Game 2 of the final, Brian Skrudland wastes little time recording the fastest overtime goal in playoff history. The Canadiens capture their 23rd Stanley Cup at the expense of the Flames. Calgary gets redemption three years later, though, beating Montreal for the franchise's only Cup.

4. Toronto 3, Montreal 2 – 1951 (2:53 of OT)

Bill Barilko scores in Game 5 – the fifth game in a row needing extra time – to clinch the Cup for the Leafs. Barilko disappears that summer when his plane goes down while returning from a fishing trip in northern Quebec. More than a decade goes by before Barilko's remains are found.

3. Montreal 3, Los Angeles 2 – 1993 (14:37 of OT)

In the Year of Overtime, when 1-in-3 games went to extra time, the Canadiens were the Team of Overtime, playing into a fourth period in 11 of 20 games. On June 7 they won their 10th overtime game setting a record likely to never be broken. Two days later, Montreal won Game 5 and captured its 24th Stanley Cup.

2. Boston 4, St. Louis 3 – 1970 (0:40 of OT)

Bobby Orr scores the Cup-clincher in Game 4 and then goes airborne, creating one of the most iconic photographs in sport. The goal gives Boston its first championship in 29 years and cements Orr's legacy as one of the most beloved sports figures in Boston history.

1. Islanders 5, Philadelphia 4 – 1980 (7:11 of OT)

Bob Nystrom swats in the series winner in Game 6 of the final for the Islanders, starting a run of four consecutive Cups for the first dynasty of the 1980s. (The Oilers are soon to follow.) 　THN

No. 1 | NY Islanders vs. Philadelphia

TORONTO
MAPLE LEAFS

Leafs Nation hates to be reminded, but it's been 45 years and counting since the Stanley Cup was last paraded down Yonge Street. And that means you won't find many (or any) Buds from recent years below.

Sorry, Mr. Sundin. Sorry, even, Mr. Sittler. You guys just didn't make the grade. Who did? This is THN's Top 10 Maple Leafs of all-time. **– JG**

10. Borje Salming

Salming was the NHL's first European superstar, doing away with the moniker 'Swedish Chickens' that was regularly used to describe Scandinavian hockey players. The rugged defenseman played through injury and insult, recording team records in assists (620) and all-star teams (six). Salming played 16 seasons with the Leafs. He's fourth all-time in points and third in games played. Hall of Fame: 1996

9. Dave Keon

Keon spent 15 seasons with the Leafs and was one of the best two-way players of his generation. Offensively the center produced 365 goals and 858 points in 1,062 games and was the team's career leader in points for 26 years until passed by Mats Sundin in 2008. Keon was a stalwart on Leafs teams that won four Cups in the 1960s. He was the NHL's rookie of the year in '61, the Lady Byng winner in '62 and '63 and the post-season MVP in '67, the last time Toronto won the Cup. HoF: 1986

8. Babe Dye

Cecil Henry Dye was a three-sport athlete during the early part of the 20th century. He played pro football with the Toronto Argonauts and was offered $25,000 by the legendary Connie Mack to join baseball's Philadelphia Athletics in 1921, but he chose to focus on hockey. Dye, a right winger who played for the then Toronto St. Patricks, led the NHL in scoring three times between 1920 and '25. He scored 176 goals in his first 170 games. Not until Wayne Gretzky joined the league some 60 years later was that pace matched. HoF: 1970

7. Ted Kennedy

'Teeder' Kennedy is known as one of the best clutch players in Maple Leafs history. A tenacious checker and faceoff wizard, Kennedy helped Toronto to five Cups in the 1940s and '50s. He was thrice named a second-team all-star and was generally considered to have hard luck in the awards department. But despite finishing 23 points behind the Art Ross winner, Kennedy won the Hart Trophy in 1955, after which he promptly retired. HoF: 1966

No. 4 | Tim Horton

6. 'Busher' Jackson

Harvey Jackson was a star on Toronto's famous 'Kid Line' during the 1930s. A pure sniper, he was first-team all-star at left wing four times in the '30s and added a second-team nod as well. Jackson led the NHL in scoring in 1931-32 and won the Hart Trophy for his troubles. That season the Leafs also won their first Cup since changing their name from the St. Pats. Jackson routinely scored 20-plus goals a season during an era when not many did. HoF: 1971

5. 'King' Clancy

Francis Clancy was a pit bull of a defenseman; a smaller player, he'd take on all comers no matter their size and, win or not, would never back down. He was acquired by the Leafs in 1930 for two players and $35,000, a monstrous sum at the time. Clancy played an exciting brand of physical, offensive hockey with top-notch defensive play thrown in the mix. During his six full years with the Leafs he was an all-star four times and won a Cup. HoF: 1958

4. Tim Horton

As strong as they came in his day, defenseman Horton was as good defensively as any player in Leafs history and had some offensive chops, to boot. During his 18 seasons with Toronto he played 1,185 games – two fewer than all-time leader George Armstrong – and sits third in career scoring by a defenseman. He died tragically in a car accident in 1974 and is most famous now for his eponymous chain of coffee shops. HoF: 1977

3. Charlie Conacher

'The Big Bomber' Conacher played the right side on Toronto's 'Kid Line' with Busher Jackson and Joe Primeau in the middle. Conacher was big for his day – 6-foot-1, 200 pounds – and used his size to bowl over anyone who got in his way. But he was skilled, too. He led the league in scoring twice in the '30s and was a five-time all-star. Like Jackson, he was a goal-scorer: 200 of his 324 points in 326 games with the Leafs came on goals. HoF: 1961

2. Frank Mahovlich

'The Big M' was billed as a prodigy coming out of junior with the St. Michael's Majors and began his career on a high, winning the Calder Trophy in 1958. The left winger scored 296 goals and 597 points with the Leafs, good for seventh all-time in team scoring. Six times during his 11 seasons with Toronto he was named an all-star, but it was never enough for management or the fans. Despite four Cups and all the accolades, Mahovlich was traded to Detroit in 1968. He played seven more NHL seasons and in the 1972 Summit Series before moving to the World Hockey Association. He was appointed to the Canadian Senate in 1998. HoF: 1981

1. Syl Apps

Charles Joseph Sylvanus Apps was a great university football player and an Olympic pole-vaulter. He's also known as the classiest guy to ever wear the Blue and White. He once offered to give back $1,000 of his $6,000 salary, because he thought he was making too much, and he enlisted in the army during World War II, costing him two years of NHL service. He was the league's rookie of the year in 1937, was a five-time all-star and won the Lady Byng Trophy in 1942 after scoring 41 points in 38 games and not taking a single penalty. His son, Syl Apps Jr., played 11 NHL seasons; grandson Syl Apps III went to Princeton on a hockey scholarship and played minor pro; and granddaughter Gillian Apps has won two Olympic gold medals with Canada and two golds and three silvers at the World Championship. HoF: 1961

No. 1 | Syl Apps

PRE-NHL PLAYERS

Before Sid The Kid, there was The Great One. Before The Great One, there was Mr. Hockey. Before Mr. Hockey, there was The Rocket.

Each of them glowed as hockey's shining star during their heyday, as did other NHLers before their time arrived. And this lineage of superstars goes back to the days before the formation of the NHL in 1917.

*In this list you will find the best of the best from the time period when pro hockey was born, the top-10 performers prior to the birth of the NHL. (Only those who never suited up for an NHL game were eligible to make this list. All stats are according to the Society of International Hockey Research.) – **BD***

10. Marty Walsh, Center

Walsh won three Stanley Cups with the Ottawa Senators, twice leading the league in scoring. His 10 goals for Ottawa in a March 16, 1911 game against Port Arthur are the second-most ever scored by a player in a Stanley Cup game.

9. Bruce Stuart, Center

The younger brother of Hod Stuart burst onto the scene with Portage Lakes, one of the founding members of the International League, hockey's first pro league, in 1903-04, scoring 44 goals in 14 regular season games and another 28 in nine playoff games. Stuart was a versatile player, capable of playing any forward position.

8. Bouse Hutton, Goal

In the days when the rules of the game prohibited netminders from leaving their feet to make a save or freeze the puck, the Ottawa Silver Seven puckstopper posted a 1.70 goals-against average in 1901-02, along with two shutouts. During the 1903 playoffs, Hutton's GAA was a stingy 1.25.

7. Ernie Russell, Center/Rover

A sensational puckhandler and finisher, Russell once scored hat tricks in five consecutive games. Including the playoffs, he tallied 54 goals in 14 games during the 1906-07 season. He scored goals in 10 straight games in 1911-12.

6. Hod Stuart, Cover Point

A towering six-footer, Stuart is considered by many hockey historians to be the sport's first great defenseman. Though known for his defense, Stuart could also attack, scoring 66 goals in 107 games.

5. Russell Bowie, Center

A five-time scoring champion, Bowie produced 266 goals in 88 career games, averaging just more than three goals per game. He scored five or more goals in a game more than a dozen times.

4. Tommy Phillips, Left/Right Winger

During the 1904-05 season, Phillips scored 31 goals in just eight games. He led the Manitoba Senior League in scoring three seasons in a row. A right-hand shot who could play either side, Phillips was among the first in hockey history to develop the strategy of driving hard to the net from his off wing.

3. Hobey Baker, Rover

An effortless skater and stickhandler, Baker was the first great American-born player. He starred at Princeton and later with the New York-based St. Nicholas club. On game days at Princeton, the marquee outside the arena simply read, "Hobey Baker plays tonight." Such was his ability that the Hockey Hall of Fame included Baker in its first induction class in 1945. The annual award for the best NCAA player bears his name.

2. Frank McGee, Center/Rover

The Ottawa Silver Seven star netted 71 goals in just 23 career games and another 66 in 22 playoff contests. On Jan. 16, 1905, McGee buried a Stanley Cup-record 14 goals as Ottawa hammered Dawson City 23-2.

1. Fred 'Cyclone' Taylor, Rover

After watching Taylor score four goals as the Ottawa Senators beat the Montreal Wanderers 4-2, Canadian governor-general Grey remarked, "That Fred Taylor is a cyclone if I ever saw one." Taylor scored 282 goals in 213 career games, capturing five scoring titles. A team from Renfrew, Ont., paid him $5,250 for a 12-game season in 1909-10. THN

DEFENSEMEN

Every ship needs a reliable anchor just like every team needs a reliable blueliner. Without that dependable, stabilizing force in the defensive end, good teams quickly become lost at sea, drifting without direction.

Whether it is a crisp first pass on the breakout, quarterbacking the point on the power play or shutting down the opponent's top line, each of the THN top 10 blueliners did it all. Some even set records that will likely never be broken. **– THN**

10. Chris Chelios, 1983-2010 – Montreal, Chicago, Detroit, Atlanta

Father time missed his appointment with Chris Chelios back in the late 1990s and darned if 'Cheli' was in any rush to re-book his date with retirement.

The youngest generation of hockey fans will remember Chelios as the aging, but remarkably fit, defensive defenseman for the Detroit Red Wings who filled a serviceable need on two Stanley Cup winners as a depth and character player.

But the real Chris Chelios was the all-around defender who was rugged, tough and dirty, offensively gifted and a defensive stalwart for many years with Montreal and Chicago.

Few players took the game more seriously or played with their heart on their sleeve as much as Chelios did for 26 seasons in the NHL. When Chelios finally retired in 2010 at the age of 48, he did so because the opportunity to play regularly had finally passed him by, not because he felt he was aging or wearing down. He fully intended on playing until the age of 50. "He was just a hockey rat; he absolutely loved the game," said San Jose Sharks GM Doug Wilson, who played in Chicago with Chelios in 1990-91. "He just loved to play hockey.

"He was intrinsically driven. Great players are highly talented people who are intrinsically driven. And that's what makes them special."

Chelios is the only player to play 400-plus games for three teams (Montreal 402, Chicago 664 and Detroit 578).

9. Paul Coffey, 1980-2001 – Edmonton, Pittsburgh, Los Angeles, Detroit, Hartford, Philadelphia, Chicago, Carolina, Boston

You could make a case that Paul Coffey was the greatest offensive defenseman ever. Unfortunately for him, we aren't ranking "offensemen."

A spectacular skater, sublime passer and fiery competitor, Coffey's reputation for his play without the puck and in his own end was spotty. Was it fair? "I don't think his defense was as bad as everyone made it out to be," said Charlie Huddy, Coffey's defense partner in Edmonton. "A lot of times a player, because of his offensive numbers, you think there has to be something that's going to be weak. And you know what? Maybe there was a bit of a lack in his defensive play and I was maybe there to help correct that, but for me it wasn't as bad as everyone made it out to be."

There's no denying Coffey's offensive brilliance. He holds the single-season mark for goals by a defenseman (48 in 1985-86) and his 138-point output that same year is one behind

No. 5 | Nicklas Lidstrom

Bobby Orr's record. Coffey is second all-time behind Ray Bourque among blueliners for career goals and points.

That he bounced around during the second half of his career, playing for seven teams in 10 campaigns (remember his 10-game stint in Chicago?), might lead you to believe he played out the string. But you'd be wrong. Coffey's desire was every bit as important as his legendary skating and passing. "That's one of the things that made him the player he was," Huddy said. "He came to play. There weren't many nights where he didn't give everything."

8. Larry Robinson, 1972-1992 – Montreal, Los Angeles

Though the memories of Larry Robinson, the Canadiens' best blueliner during their dominating dynasty of the late 1970s, are plentiful, perhaps none stands out more than his taming of the 'Broad Street Bullies.'

During the 1976 final, Robinson, a 6-foot-4, 225-pounder nicknamed 'Big Bird,' beat down notorious tough guy Dave 'The Hammer' Schultz during a line brawl and in the process proved the Habs would not be intimated by the two-time defending champs. "He was physically dominant," said 1982 Norris winner and current Sharks GM Doug Wilson, who won the 1984 Canada Cup with Robinson. "When the Canadiens would go into Philly, he would take care of business. He could do everything."

And he could do everything very well. Robinson was a complete player who dominated in all three zones, as attested by his NHL career record plus-730. He's also one of only two NHLers, along with Bobby Orr, to put up a single-season rating greater than plus-100, when he posted an astounding plus-120 in 1976-77, the year he won the first of his two Norris Trophies.

But while Robinson, inducted into the Hall of Fame in 1995 and slotted No. 7 in *Habs Heroes*, THN's 2008 list of the greatest Canadiens of all-time, was as tough as they come, he left any pugilistic predisposition on the ice. "Forget about him being one of the greatest players to have ever played the game," Wilson said, "Larry is one of the greatest people I've ever met in my life."

7. Red Kelly, 1947-1967 – Detroit, Toronto

Even though Red Kelly's junior career was spent with the St. Michael's Majors, a Maple Leafs pipeline team, his NHL career started with Detroit after a Leafs scout said Kelly wouldn't make it as an NHLer.

But, as a 20-year-old, Kelly began his NHL career as the fifth defenseman, before being moved up the depth chart in Year 2 thanks to a little fate. "(Doug) 'Crash' McCaig broke his leg and I became the fourth defenseman and they saw I was capable of doing the work, so when 'Crash' got better they traded him to Chicago," said Kelly.

One of the most versatile players of all-time, Kelly was known for his checking abilities and puckhandling skills. Though he wasn't a banger, Kelly was the inaugural winner of the Norris Trophy for the NHL's best defenseman in 1954. He was also runner-up that season for the Hart Trophy.

After winning four Cups in Detroit, the team traded him to the Maple Leafs. "I was going to show them they made a mistake," Kelly said.

Toronto coach Punch Imlach moved Kelly, who played forward from time to time in Detroit, to center. The Leafs knew all roads to the Cup went through Montreal and they needed a smart pivot to check the great Jean Beliveau. "It's hockey, that's all; it's just a different position," Kelly said of the change.

Kelly won another four Stanley Cups with Toronto and reached the 20-goal plateau three times before retiring after the Maple Leafs' 1967 Cup triumph.

6. Denis Potvin, 1973-1988 – Islanders

In 15 NHL seasons, he scored almost a point per game. He once finished seventh in the NHL scoring race with 101 points. And he was the first blueliner to reach 1,000 career points. But ask Denis Potvin about his favorite aspect of hockey and you won't hear much about offense.

"I really enjoyed the physical part of the game," the long-time Islanders captain said, "setting the tone with a big hit and distracting the other team. It was something I remember my coaches stressing when I was a kid."

A seven-time all-star, Potvin scored 20-plus goals nine times and averaged better than a point per game on eight occasions. But of the 10 highest-scoring D-men all-time – Potvin is No. 6 – only Chris Chelios averaged more penalty minutes per game. Potvin's career plus-460 ranking is third all-time among blueliners.

To put it simply: Potvin could play it any way. He could skate, had a big shot, was slick with the disc, had great vision and beat guys in the trenches, at both ends of the ice. Those talents helped him lead the Islanders to four consecutive Cups.

After a career filled with individual accolades and awards, Potvin was a first-ballot Hall of Famer in 1991 and soon became a television analyst. But ask him what personal achievement he's most proud of from his playing days and he responds like the prototypical hockey player he was: "You don't dream about those things growing up, you dream about getting to the NHL and winning the Stanley Cup."

5. Nicklas Lidstrom, 1991-2012 – Detroit

Nicklas Lidstrom laughed when asked to name the best part of his nuanced game. "It's hard to talk about yourself that way," he said sheepishly.

It's even harder when you're the best defenseman of your generation. The holes in Lidstrom's game were few, if any. He was not the most physical, didn't have the biggest shot and wasn't renowned for his skating. But his skill set was sublime, beginning with his smarts. "My positioning is one of the reasons I made it this far," he said. "Trying to be in the right spot at the right time makes everything so much easier."

Lidstrom was one of those guys who made everyone around him better. Whether it was point shots off the end boards to create scoring chances, angling players off the puck or just his cool, collected demeanor under pressure, players loved to play with him.

Hall of Famer Luc Robitaille won a Stanley Cup with Lidstrom in Detroit. He remembers being taken aback by Steve Yzerman saying Lidstrom was the best player he'd ever played with and had never seen him play a bad game. "Even Wayne Gretzky had bad games, everybody has bad games," Robitaille recalled thinking at the time. "To this day, I've never seen Nick Lidstrom have a bad game. It's amazing...for him a bad game would be one bad pass."

And when was the last time you saw Lidstrom make a bad pass?

No. 1 | Bobby Orr

4. Ray Bourque, 1979-2000 – Boston, Colorado

Beginning with his Calder Trophy-winning debut in 1979-80 and culminating in the victory of a Stanley Cup more than 20 years later, long-time Bruins stalwart Ray Bourque was as adept at shutting down goal-scorers as he was producing offense.

His accolades include five Norris Trophies, 13 first-team all-star selections, six second-team distinctions and more points than any other defenseman in NHL history. Bourque's best campaign came in 1983-84, when he posted 31 goals and 96 points, both career highs.

While he played on some excellent squads, Bourque never won a Cup in Beantown. The Bruins made the final twice during Bourque's time there, losing to the Oilers in 1988 and 1990. Bourque was nearing the end without a ring.

Having been a loyal soldier in Boston, no one faulted him for asking to be traded to a contender. The Bruins dealt Bourque to Colorado in 2000 to play alongside Joe Sakic, Peter Forsberg and Patrick Roy. The Avs fell short of the goal, but Bourque would not be deterred. Soon to be 40, he decided to give it one more season. "There wasn't any debate," Bourque said. "I knew I had plenty left in the tank. It was unfinished business, but I knew it was going to be my last year."

Bourque and the Avs accomplished their goal by dispatching New Jersey in a seven-game final. Sakic made sure Bourque was the first teammate to hoist the Cup after him. "He was so excited for me and for me touching the Cup," Bourque said.

3. Eddie Shore, 1926-1940 – Boston, New York Americans

Take Paul Coffey's skating ability, Chris Pronger's nastiness, Nick Lidstrom's ability to defend, Zdeno Chara's endurance and Ed Belfour's idiosyncratic personality and roll it up into one early 20th century player. There you have Eddie Shore.

That Shore was one of the greatest players of his era is beyond dispute. No defenseman has won as many as Shore's four Hart Trophies. Had the NHL recognized the league's best defenseman during his era, Shore would have an armful of Norris Trophies to his credit as well. "The best way you can put it," said hockey historian Eric Zweig, "is he was actually the best rushing defenseman of his era, the best defensive defenseman and the toughest defenseman."

That combination of skill and guile made Shore one of the most feared players of his time in any area of the ice. But Shore also had a dark side. He was a violent player who almost took the life of Toronto star Ace Bailey when he clubbed Bailey with his stick in 1933. He was also an eccentric loner and even teammates often steered clear. He refused to wear suspenders because he said they affected his breathing, cut the blade of his stick short and wore the same skates almost his entire career.

His impact on the ice, however, was never in doubt. "Our coach Art Ross told me: 'The reason I play Shore so much is because the opposition knows how great he is and they concentrate on Shore and leave the rest of you alone,' " said Hall of Famer Milt Schmidt.

2. Doug Harvey, 1947-1969 – Montreal, Rangers, Detroit

Before Bobby Orr, there was Doug Harvey. Both carved their legends as their eras' respective defenseman-without-peer. Both were no-brainers for the Hall of Fame. Both played the majority of their careers for Original Six franchises. But the similarities end there.

Injuries limited Orr to 12 seasons, while Harvey played 24 years. And their on-ice styles differed. "Where Orr controlled (the game) by carrying the puck, by acting as a forward, Harvey would slow the pace down, then pick it up," said Kevin Shea, hockey historian.

For 14 years, he was a key component on the Habs attack – and a member of six Stanley Cup-winning squads. "Harvey did what was expected of him," said Hall of Famer Dick Duff. "He was nobody's fool. He was a smart player, someone tough who didn't mind mixing it up. We all knew we had to bring our best to have a chance of beating him."

Harvey was named to the NHL all-star team 11 consecutive years. He won the Norris Trophy seven times in eight seasons. He accomplished those things while living a boozy off-ice existence and directing energy to the creation of the NHL Players' Association in 1957.

Harvey's later years were marred by homelessness and alcoholism and, ultimately, his death from cirrhosis of the liver in 1989. "At the end, people hung on to his past glories," Shea said. "He wasn't taking care of himself, but he still had innate knowledge that made him, if not dominant, then a good player. In its own way, that's impressive."

1. Bobby Orr, 1966-1979 – Boston, Chicago

When you talk to Bobby Orr, there isn't a lot of new stuff to cover. His days as the best defenseman of all-time are well documented.

There is plenty to suggest Orr's record for points in a season by a defenseman, 139, could stand the test of time. Joe Malone's seven goals in a game hasn't been unequalled for more than 80 years and that's how long it could be before anyone matches Orr.

Orr said the seeds of his game were sowed on the river in Parry Sound, Ont., where no coach could tell him to stay back and there were no boards for chip passes. "It was, 'Just drop the puck and let's play,' " Orr said.

There is little doubt he was the most dynamic skater to ever patrol a blueline. He had the ability to change a game. Orr won three straight Hart Trophies and eight consecutive Norris Trophies. "(We) were allowed into the offensive zone," Orr said. "It also helped that we had an incredible power play."

But he worries now about today's approach to the game. "We get some coaches teaching the trap. Are you (kidding) me?" Orr said. "It all comes back to the kids, letting the kids do it early on. And I'm sure the pro influences the kid, the same way I probably had some influence on kids."

To be sure, Orr helped spawn a generation of offensive defensemen from Denis Potvin to Paul Coffey to Larry Murphy to Ray Bourque. "It was a game to me, it wasn't work," Orr said. "It was my dream and my dream came true. ᴛʜɴ

LONGEST
TEAM STREAKS

Every season it never fails: at least one team goes on a monumental winning streak to vault up the standings, while some other poor chumps go on a regrettable and forgettable losing run that kills their season. Some of those stretches, however, go down in the annals.

We here at THN award success more than futility, so winning and undefeated streaks get precedence over losing and winless streaks. – JG

No. 6 | Pittsburgh Penguins, 1992-93

10. Philadelphia Quakers, 1930-31, 15 consecutive losses

The Quakers lasted just one NHL season, finishing with a paltry .136 winning percentage (4-36-4) in 44 games. Gerry Lowrey led the team in scoring with 13 goals and 27 points. The league leader was Montreal's Howie Morenz with 28 goals and 51 points.

9. New York Islanders, 1981-82, 15 consecutive victories
The Islanders were at the height of their power in '81-82. They finished first overall with a 54-16-10 record and won their third of four Stanley Cups in May, losing just four playoff games along the way.

8. San Jose Sharks, 1992-93, 17 consecutive losses
In just their second season, the Sharks finished with an 11-71-2 record (a record for single-season losses). Amazingly, however, they finished just second last overall; Ottawa also finished with 24 points, but had one fewer victory. San Jose did manage to give up the most goals in the league, though, a mind-boggling 414 or 4.9 per game, and tie the mark for most consecutive losses. Not a single player finished with a plus rating. Three finished minus-50.

7. Washington Capitals, 1974-75, 17 consecutive losses
Known as the worst team of all-time, the expansion Capitals finished with an 8-67-5 record, 20 points behind the next worst team, Kansas City. Washington set or tied the modern records for fewest wins in a season, fewest road wins (one), fewest points (21), most consecutive losses and most goals allowed (446).

6. Pittsburgh Penguins, 1992-93, 17 consecutive victories
The Penguins were coming off two Stanley Cup parades and boasted a lineup that included scoring leader Mario Lemieux (69 goals, 160 points in 60 games), eventual No. 4 all-time career scorer Ron Francis, power forwards Kevin Stevens and Rick Tocchet (103 goals, 220 points combined) Hall of Fame defenseman Larry Murphy (fifth-most blueliner points ever) and top netminder Tom Barrasso. And they were coached by Scotty Bowman. The Pens won the Presidents' Trophy with a 56-21-7 record and set the mark for consecutive wins, but fell in the second round to the Islanders in seven games.

5. Washington Capitals, 1975-76, 25-game winless streak
Ah those loveable Caps. Turns out Year 2 wasn't much better than Year 1: An 11-59-10 record, last overall by four points and a minus-170 goal differential. But they did tie the modern record for fewest home wins (6). Their leading scorer was Nelson Pyatt with 26 goals and 49 points, 76 behind league leader Guy Lafleur.

4. Kansas City Scouts, 1975-76, 27-game winless streak
Wow. When the NHL expanded in the '70s, it really didn't ice competitive squads. The '75-76 season set the mark for futility. The Scouts lasted just two seasons before moving to Colorado to become the Rockies until '86 and then off to New Jersey, where they remain the Devils. Unlike the hapless Caps, the hapless Scouts were actually worse their second season, finishing with a 12-56-12 record.

3. Montreal Canadiens, 1977-78, 28-game undefeated streak

The Habs were, um, OK in the '70s. They won six Cups, including four in a row to finish the decade. They also racked up three Art Ross Trophies, two Harts, two Mastertons, five Vezinas, a Calder, four Conn Smythes, a Norris, two Selkes, three Pearsons and a Jack Adams Award. Montreal finished first overall in '77-78 with a 59-10-11 record and finished plus-176 in goal differential.

2. Winnipeg Jets, 1980-81, 30-game winless streak

Only one team has won fewer games than the '80-81 Jets, who finished with a 9-57-14 record. Winnipeg finished last overall by 24 points. Interestingly, the Jets won 20 games the season before (their first after being absorbed from the World Hockey Association) and 33 the season after (Dale Hawerchuk's rookie year), showing the volatility of NHL hockey in the early '80s.

1. Philadelphia Flyers, 1979-80, 35-game undefeated streak

The Broad Street Bullies had seven players finish the season with 100-plus penalty minutes, but they could do a lot more than just bang and crash. Their 48-12-20 record was good for first overall and they lost just two playoff games on their way to the final, where the Islanders won their first of four consecutive Cups. Ken Linseman (79 points), Reggie Leach (50 goals) and goaltender Pete Peeters (29-5-5, 2.73 GAA) led the Flyers. THN

No. 1 | Philadelphia Flyers, 1979-80

NO. 1 NHL
DRAFT PICKS

The first player taken No. 1 in the NHL entry draft was winger Garry Monahan in 1963, a 16-year-old from the St. Michael's Juveniles in Toronto who never became a star.

In the 46 years since the NHL instituted the draft, there have been a number of flops, the most famous being Montreal's selection of Doug Wickenheiser over Denis Savard in 1980 and Ottawa choosing Alexandre Daigle in 1993, rather than Chris Pronger or Paul Kariya.

On the flip side, there are players who have gone on to have legendary careers and will never be forgotten. Here are THN's Top 10 No. 1 NHL picks. – JG

No. 9 | Mats Sundin, 1989

10. Eric Lindros, 1991

His inability to stay healthy is what keeps Lindros from being higher on this list. At his peak, big No. 88 was the most physically dominating player in the world, along with being one of the most skilled. He averaged more than a point per game during his career – much of which came at the height of the Dead Puck Era – including nearly a goal every two games. In 1995, Lindros won the Hart Trophy and the Lester Pearson Award. He also captained Team Canada at the 1998 Nagano Olympics, the year NHLers debuted at the Winter Games. No. 2 after Lindros, Pat Falloon, had 322 career NHL points.

9. Mats Sundin, 1989

The first European to be taken No. 1 overall, Sundin didn't win any major awards or a Stanley Cup, but is 27th all-time in NHL scoring and was a trailblazer for teenaged prospects from across the pond. No. 2 after Sundin, Dave Chyzowski, had 31 career NHL points.

8. Mike Modano, 1988

The highest-scoring American-born player of all-time, Modano is 23rd on the NHL's career scoring list. He had 13 25-plus goal seasons and eight 80-plus point years. He won a Cup with Dallas in 1999 and also played for the United States nine times in senior men's competition. The No. 2 selection in 1988, Trevor Linden, had 867 career NHL points.

7. Alex Ovechkin, 2004

His production has dipped over the past two seasons, but two Hart Trophies, an Art Ross, two Rocket Richard Trophies and two Lester Pearson Awards before the age of 27 is nothing to sneeze at. No. 2 in 2004 was fellow Russian Evgeni Malkin, who has 527 career points, 152 less than Ovie's 679.

6. Sidney Crosby, 2005

Crosby, too, has won the Art Ross and Hart Trophies and the Lester Pearson Award, though just once each. But, as Ovechkin said, "Cups is Cups" and that's why Sid's Stanley Cup ring from 2009 puts him one spot ahead on this list. Bobby Ryan, drafted No. 2 that year, has 259 career NHL points to date, a mere 350 behind Crosby's 609.

5. Gilbert Perreault, 1970

Perreault was a member of the famed 'French Connection' line in Buffalo during the 1970s and played for Canada at the 1972 Summit Series, after just two years in the NHL. He later starred as Wayne Gretzky's linemate at the 1981 Canada Cup. Perreault was the main building block for the expansion Buffalo Sabres and finished his career with 1,326 points in 1,191 games. He won the 1971 Calder Trophy and the 1973 Lady Byng Trophy. No. 2 after Perreault, Dale Tallon, had 336 career NHL points.

4. Guy Lafleur, 1971

One of the most charismatic players in NHL history, Lafleur was the best player in the world for a period during the 1970s. Between 1976 and 1978 he won three-straight Art Ross Trophies and Lester Pearson Awards, two Hart Trophies, a Conn Smythe Trophy and, over his whole career, five Stanley Cups. Known as 'The Flower', Lafleur is 26th all-time in NHL scoring with 1353 points. No. 2 after Lafleur, Marcel Dionne, had 1,771 career points, good for fifth all-time.

3. Dale Hawerchuk, 1981

With 1,409 points, Hawerchuk ranks 18th all-time in NHL scoring. He was forever in the shadow of Gretzky, but remains one of the most skilled players ever. Hawerchuk won the

Calder Trophy in 1982 after a 103-point season, his fourth-highest point total of his career. He still holds the record for assists in one period with five. No. 2 after Hawerchuk, Doug Smith, had 253 career NHL points.

2. Denis Potvin, 1973

The third blueliner to go first overall, Potvin was also the best. He's the sixth-highest scoring defenseman in NHL history and only Bobby Orr and Paul Coffey have better PPG averages among the leaders. He was the first blueliner in NHL history to top 300 goals and 1,000 points. Oh, he also won four Stanley Cups with the Islanders, the 1974 Calder Trophy, three Norris Trophies and was the Hart Trophy runner-up in 1976. No. 2 after Potvin, Tom Lysiak, had 843 career NHL points.

1. Mario Lemieux, 1984

Lemieux was the biggest slam-dunk in NHL draft history, notching 133 goals and 282 points in 70 Quebec League games during his draft year. Lemieux went on to a legendary career stymied somewhat by health problems. He is seventh all-time in NHL scoring with 690 goals and 1,723 points in 915 games. Among the top-60 NHL scorers, only Peter Stastny and Mike Bossy have played less than 1,000 games – they're Nos. 36 and 52. Lemieux won the Calder Trophy, six Art Ross Trophies, four Lester Pearson Awards, three Hart Trophies, two Conn Smythe Trophies, a Masterton Trophy and led the Penguins to back-to-back Stanley Cups in 1991 and '92. He was also a legendary international player for Canada, particularly making his mark alongside Gretzky during the 1987 Canada Cup. THN

No. 1 | Mario Lemieux, 1984

HOCKEY COUPLES

Most, if not all, professional hockey players are in love with the game. But that doesn't mean there's no room in their lives for another love.
Who are the greatest famous hockey couples of all-time? – AP

No. 8 | Hilary Duff & Mike Comrie

10. Valeri Bure and Candace Cameron

The retired right winger, who spent a decade in the NHL, and the former star of *Full House* have been married since 1996, which can be an eternity for pro athlete marriages. They're as strong as ever, however, and even own the Bure Family Wines, which was founded in 2007.

9. Bret Hedican and Kristi Yamaguchi

Hedican won a Stanley Cup in Carolina during his 17-year NHL career. Yamaguchi won an Olympic gold medal in figure skating in 1992 and won the sixth season of *Dancing With The Stars*. If they ever entered *Battle of the Blades,* they'd win running (or skating) away.

8. Mike Comrie and Hilary Duff

Comrie retired from the NHL in February of 2012 and no doubt is looking forward to spending more time with his singer/actress wife, who he married in 2010. The couple welcomed their first child – Luca Cruz Comrie – into the world in March of 2012.

7. Sergei Fedorov and Anna Kournikova

In 2003, The Hockey News was the first to reveal the secret, short-lived marriage between the long-time Red Wings center and the tennis superstar. He captained Metallurg of the Kontinental League in 2011-12, while she has been with singer Enrique Iglesias for more than a decade.

6. Mike Fisher and Carrie Underwood

Fisher began dating *American Idol* superstar Underwood while still playing for the Ottawa Senators and the pair married in 2010. When Fisher was dealt to Nashville, the match became even more perfect, what with Underwood's near-godlike status in the country music community.

5. Alexei Yashin and Carol Alt

American supermodel Alt was once married to another hockey star (long-time Ranger Ron Greschner), but after the duo divorced, she fell in love with Islanders mainstay Alexei Yashin and the couple has been together since 2000.

4. Ray Ferraro and Cammi Granato

Easily the duo with the most hockey talent on this list, the former NHLer (and current TSN analyst) and women's hockey legend were married in 2004. They have two young sons, Riley and Reese, both of whom should be considered odds-on favorites for NHL careers when they come of age.

3. Don and Rose Cherry

The legendary coach and his wife arguably were Canada's most famous couple until her death in 1997. Don Cherry founded Rose Cherry's Home For Kids (since renamed Darling Home For Kids) in Milton, Ont., to help care for seriously ill children.

2. Wayne Gretzky and Janet Jones

When the game's biggest name married the Hollywood actress in Edmonton in 1988, the news coverage was something you'd expect to see for a royal wedding. In the hockey world, that's exactly what it was – and the still-married pair has produced five kids, including budding baseball star Trevor, who signed with the Chicago Cubs in 2011.

1. Gordie and Colleen Howe

If the measure of a love affair is how well a couple cares for one another in the tough times of their marriage, the Howes have shown us all how it's done. Not only did they raise a hockey-playing brood that included Hall-of-Famer Mark Howe and WHA/NHL veteran Marty Howe, but when Colleen was stricken with the debilitating Pick's Disease in 2002, Gordie looked after her until she passed away in 2009 at age 76. As phenomenal a player as Gordie was, he was a Hall of Fame husband, too. 📰

No. 1 | Gordie & Colleen Howe

NEW YORK RANGERS

As one of the NHL's Original Six, the New York Rangers have employed a cavalcade of stars over the years, including Barry Beck, Ron Greschner, Frank Boucher, Ron Duguay, and Pavel Bure.

But for as fantastic as they were, those five didn't make it into the pantheon of the 10 best Blueshirts in franchise history. They are... **– AP**

No. 6 | Andy Bathgate

10. Vic Hadfield

A rugged left winger and captain from 1971-74, Hadfield was the first Ranger to score 50 goals in a season. The Oakville, Ont., native's 262 career goals as a member of the Blueshirts put him fifth overall in franchise history.

9. Jean Ratelle

During a two-decade NHL career, the Lac-Saint-Jean, Que., native earned a spot in the Hockey Hall of Fame in 1985 via his incredible consistency in producing offense. All but six of the center's 20 seasons were spent in Manhattan and he held the team record for points in a single season (109 in 1971-72) until Jaromir Jagr posted 123 in 2005-06. Hall of Fame: 1985

8. Harry Howell

After joining the Blueshirts in 1952, Howell played 1,160 games for the team, more than any other player in franchise history. The stay-at-home defenseman had just 94 goals and 418 points in 1,411 career NHL games (all but 251 of which were as a Ranger) and played in just 38 playoff games, yet his defensive prowess was recognized with induction into the Hall of Fame. HoF: 1979

7. Adam Graves

When he arrived in Manhattan in 1991, Graves' personal statistics took off as the team's fortunes improved: he set the franchise record for goals in a season when he netted 52 in 1993-94, the same season he scored 10 goals and 17 points in the playoffs and helped lead the team to its first Cup in 54 years.

6. Andy Bathgate

The first two-thirds of Bathgate's 18 years in the NHL were played as a Ranger and he did not disappoint, winning a Hart Trophy as league MVP in 1958-59. Bathgate had 729 points in 719 games, making him the only one of the franchise's all-time top 20 scorers to average a point per game. HoF: 1978

5. Ed Giacomin

Hailing from Sudbury, Ont., Giacomin broke through as a dominant star in his second season and went on to lead the league three times in shutouts while sharing a Vezina Trophy with teammate Gilles Villemure in 1971. He still holds the team record for shutouts (49) and with 266 wins he is second only to Mike Richter. HoF: 1987

4. Mike Richter

The Abington, Pa., native is one of the greatest American-born goalies in history and holds the Rangers' records for wins (301) and games played by a goalie (666), but it was Richter's mastery of the Blueshirts' Cup-winning 1993-94 season that seals his lofty spot. That year, he set a Rangers record for single-season wins (42) that still stands and led the team to the Presidents' Trophy.

3. Rod Gilbert

The right winger and native Montrealer spent all of his 16 NHL seasons as a Blueshirt. He's the first and only NHLer to score 1,000 or more points as a Ranger (1,021) and scored at least 25 goals in each of his final seven full seasons. Small wonder he was, in 1979, the first Ranger to have his number retired. HoF: 1982

2. Mark Messier

Whether it was the immediate impact he made when he became a Ranger in 1991 – amassing 35 goals and 107 points while changing the culture of the dressing room – or his unforgettable play in the 1994 playoffs, Messier's near superhuman force of will and leadership resonates in Manhattan and across the hockey world to this day. HoF: 2007

1. Brian Leetch

Leetch's skill on the Rangers blueline over 17 of his 18 NHL seasons was nearly unparalleled by any defenseman of his generation. He won two Norris Trophies, was named team MVP six times, holds a slew of Rangers records, including assists (741) and most assists in one season (80), and was the first American-born player to win the Conn Smythe Trophy when the Blueshirts won it all in 1994. Tough to top that act. HoF: 2009 ᴛʜɴ

No. 1 | Brian Leetch

WAYNE GRETZKY
ACHIEVEMENTS

When he was inducted into the Hockey Hall of Fame in 1999, Wayne Gretzky said, "In 10 years, players will be better than I was."

More than a decade later, that prediction represents one of the few times in life Gretzky didn't get it right.

Virtually all of the dozens of NHL records The Great One set over his 20-year career remain intact. In honor of Gretzky, here are his top 10 hockey achievements. – AP

10. Kid wonderful

As a 4-foot-10 novice player in his hometown of Brantford, Ont., Gretzky amasses 378 goals and 517 points for the Nadrofsky Steelers.

9. Junior mint

In 1977-78 as a member of the Sault Ste. Marie Greyhounds, Gretzky sets the Ontario League's single-season record for goals by a 16-year-old with 70. (The record stood until 2006-07, when John Tavares scored 72 for the Oshawa Generals.)

8. 50-20 vision

On April 2, 1980, at the age of 19 years, two months and seven days, Gretzky nets his 50th goal – making him the youngest player in NHL history to hit the half-hundred mark.

7. A sixth sensation

As a 23-year-old, Gretzky hits the 1,000-point mark in only his sixth NHL season.

6. Seventh heaven

In what he called the greatest game of his career, Gretzky records a hat trick and adds an assist for good measure in his Kings' 5-4 victory over Toronto in Game 7 of the 1993 Campbell Conference final.

5. Howe about that?

On March 29, 1999, Gretzky scores the final goal of his career, against the New York Islanders. The goal was his 1,072nd WHA/NHL goal (regular season and playoffs), breaking Gordie Howe's record of 1,071.

4. A case in points

In April of 1986, Gretzky records his 215th point of the regular season – his highest career total and the fourth time he broke the 200-point mark – to set an NHL record that remains to this day.

No. 10 | Minor Hockey Star

No. 5 | Last Career Goal

3. Important to set goals

In a February, 1982 game against Buffalo, Gretzky scores his 77th goal of the season to break Phil Esposito's single-season record. He finishes the season with a career-best (and still NHL-record) 92 goals in 80 games.

2. That's too grand

At age 29, Gretzky becomes the only player in league history to reach the 2,000-point plateau by notching an assist in an Oct. 26, 1990 game. When he retires nine years later with 2,857 points in 1,487 career games, he will have 970 more points than the next-highest scorer (Mark Messier, with 1,887 in 1,756 games).

1. He's the boss

On Dec. 30, 1981, Gretzky scores five goals against Philadelphia; the fifth was his 50th of the season, in just his 39th game, obliterating the previous NHL record of 50 goals in 50 games (first set by Maurice 'Rocket' Richard in 1944-45 and equalled by Mike Bossy in 1980-81). THN

NHLERS ON TWITTER

In the dog days of summer you can't follow your favorite NHL players on the ice. But thanks to the rise of social media, that doesn't mean you can't follow them off it. Here are the best NHLers to follow on Twitter. – AP

No. 9 | Taylor Hall

10. Mike Commodore (@Commie22)

After spending the majority of 2010-11 in the American League, Commodore was back in the NHL in 2011-12, splitting time between Detroit and Tampa Bay. He's as self-deprecating, honest and funny as anyone in the game. **Sample Tweet:** "It's confirmed...Chris Bosh was crying in the hallway...wow. I know losing in the finals sucks but keep it together till no cameras around."

9. Taylor Hall (@Hallsy04)

Edmonton's young star uses Twitter as any youngster would: as part confessional, part joking buddy, part flirting zone and part teammate-chirping assister. **Sample Tweet:** "Getting poked by guys on Facebook is just straight up weird"

8. Bobby Ryan (@B_Ryan9)

The Ducks star right winger is usually fun-loving and polite to people with whom he interacts. But he's not above answering his critics or giving a former teammate the business. **Sample Tweet:** "You look like a scarecrow and a condor mated."

7. Logan Couture (@Logancouture)

Couture is mature beyond his years and clearly is having fun in the Twitter world, sometimes at the expense of his brethren. **Sample Tweet:** "Trying to find footage of Jamal Mayers' (@jamalmayers) first NHL goal. Did they have cameras back in 98-99? If so, is it black and white?"

6. Jaromir Jagr (@68Jagr)

He only recently began personally tweeting on his official account, but the future Hockey Hall of Famer has quickly established his tweets as must-reads. For instance, take his line after Flyers teammate Ilya Bryzgalov joked that he was only scared of bears and a number of Pittsburgh Penguins fans dressed up as the furry beasts for their 2012 first round playoff series. **Sample Tweet:** "Bryz is scared of bears. There were like 70 bears at the game! I wonder what would happen if he said he is scared of beautiful naked girls?!"

5. David Perron (@DP_57)

Perron was plagued with a concussion for most of 2010-11, but remains one of the brightest young talented players in the league, proven by his performance in 2011-12. He doesn't mind making his opinions known. **Sample Tweet:** "For those who say (Alex) Kovalev didn't care, you are NOT born with skills and finesse like that, you work at it, and he sure did!!!"

4. Joffrey Lupul (@JLupul)

One of the more well-travelled names on this list, Lupul is more intelligent than the average NHLer and is as passionate about music and other sports as he is about hockey. **Sample Tweet:** "Foster The People or Eddie Vedder tonight?? Tough call."

3. Ryan Whitney (@RyanWhitney6)

The Oilers D-man has something to say about sports and entertainment issues and doesn't care who knows it. **Sample Tweet:** "I can't believe the Patriots traded for possibly the laziest, biggest idiot in pro sports. Albert Haynesworth is a slob."

2. Ilya Bryzgalov (@BryzGoalie30)

The Flyers goalie had a roller coaster first season in Philadelphia and among his challenges was to rein in his colorful persona. Anyone who's seen his entertaining musings on Twitter would surely hope he doesn't pull back his personality too far. He doesn't tweet often, but when he does, his followers see him as the most interesting man in the hockey world. **Sample Tweet:** "Why Canadians so aggressive on twitter?"

1. Paul Bissonnette (@BizNasty2Point0)

The Vito Corleone of players on Twitter, 'BizNasty' can get a bit raunchy, but he's a good-natured dude and knows his role online and on the ice. **Sample Tweet:** "If you wear sunglasses in a club, you're a loser." THN

No. 1 | Paul Bissonnette

CENTERS

Teams that can find a dominant player up the middle will hold on to him for dear life. When they don't, they regret it. On the other side of the spectrum, teams left out in the cold without that powerful pivot, long for the warmth that a No. 1 center provides.

The players who follow have one thing in common: they each provided game-breaking abilities that contributed significantly to their respective team's success. — *THN*

No. 6 | Stan Mikita

10. Joe Sakic, 1988-2009 – Quebec/Colorado

It was the ninth inning of Joe Sakic's career and The Hockey News conducted a poll among NHL players. "Who's the most respected player in the game?" we asked.

No surprise Sakic won, but the landslide verdict was a stirring tribute to 'Burnaby Joe' or 'Gentleman Joe.' "Joe Sakic was a classic elite centerman, a smaller version of Jean Beliveau who brought so much class and dignity to the position and the sport," said Hall of Famer Bobby Clarke.

Sakic was intense on the ice and found another gear on the rush before unleashing the generation's most potent wrist shot. He retired in 2009 ranked 14th in goals, 11th in assists and eighth in points, spending his entire career with one franchise.

Ex-teammate Ray Bourque recalls Sakic's quiet leadership and intensity to achieve success. "I remember heading into New Jersey for Game 6 (of the 2001 Stanley Cup final) and nobody gave us a chance," Bourque said. "We won 4-0 and on the trip home, Joe was chasing me all over the plane: 'How are we going to do this?' 'How are we going to do what, Joe?' I asked. 'How are we going to do the hand-off when we win the Stanley Cup?' I said, 'Let's play the game first.' "

Clarke respects Sakic for what he wasn't. "A lot of us were successful, but we were rats on the ice, too; we did a lot of dirty stuff," Clarke said. "But Sakic had a class about him. He never shied away from anything, but never got into the ratty stuff that many of us did."

9. Bobby Clarke, 1969-1984 – Philadelphia

In addition to his impressive and thorough skill set, one Wayne Gretzky said he attempted to emulate, Clarke was renowned for his work ethic.

But if you ask him, any praise in that regard is misplaced. "If you're defined for working hard, it just means the other guys weren't," said Clarke, a diabetic since youth. "For me it wasn't working hard, it was doing it properly."

Whatever it was, it helped him become a legend not only in Philadelphia, but in the annals of hockey history. A better playmaker than goal-scorer, Clarke, rated No. 24 in THN's 1997 list of The Top 100 Players of All-Time, twice led the NHL in assists and averaged 1.06 points per game during his 15-year career. His game, however, was about much more than numbers. He was a tenacious backchecker, a demon in the faceoff circle and one of the game's great leaders, spending 12 season's as Flyers captain.

Durability was also one of his key traits – he only once played fewer than 70 games in a season – something he attributes to never wilting on the ice. "I knew how to play and I knew how to protect myself," Clarke said. "I wasn't afraid to hurt somebody if they were out to hurt me and I think that type of attitude buys you space out there. A lot of guys didn't want to go after me because they knew I'd take my stick to them if they did."

Regrettably, for some it's that stickwork, specifically on Valeri Kharlamov in 1972 Summit Series, that overshadows his breadth of accomplishments.

8. Steve Yzerman, 1983-2006 – Detroit

Steve Yzerman operated with one defining cause during his sensational NHL career, a fact Detroit Red Wings coach Mike Babcock neatly summed up upon the announcement of Yzerman's retirement in 2006.

"He just does the right thing time in and time out, even when the right thing is very hard to do," Babcock said. "Most of us go for the path of least resistance. That's not Steve Yzerman. He was always about the team."

Detroit's captain and unquestioned leader for more than two decades, Yzerman was an athlete admired as much for his courage and leadership as for his ample skill. "When I think of

Steve, I think of competitiveness and intensity," said Detroit assistant GM Jim Nill. "The will to win. He was going to win no matter what."

Yzerman sought no part of individual glory. Even his 2009 induction into the Hockey Hall of Fame left Yzerman feeling sheepish. "It does feel strange to be considered a Hall of Famer," Yzerman said. "Growing up and really being in the league, you run into the Hall of Famers, you would see them on TV, see the names and it's a pretty awesome group."

He was entirely comfortable with his 2006 decision to walk away from playing for reasons that would be expected from 'Stevie Y.' "The determining factor was that I wasn't going to be able to do the things I feel are necessary to play a role on the team," said Yzerman, now the GM of the Tampa Bay Lightning.

7. Phil Esposito, 1963-1981 – Chicago, Boston, Rangers

A popular bumper sticker in the Boston area in the 1970s read: "Jesus saves, Espo scores on the rebound."

Phil Esposito, a big, powerful center who liked to park himself in front of the net and bang away at rebounds, took offense to a new dimension in the decade before Wayne Gretzky. He was the first NHLer to eclipse 100 points, for Boston in 1968-69, then two years later erupted for an unheard of 76 goals and 152 points.

Centering a line with Wayne Cashman and Ken Hodge that became known as 'The Nitro Line,' the 6-foot-1, 205-pounder won five Art Ross Trophies and two Hart Trophies as the game exploded offensively when the NHL expanded from six teams to 12.

The powerhouse Bruins won Cups in 1970 and '72, but in '75 Esposito was traded to the New York Rangers. "At the time it was devastating," Esposito said. "I felt like my whole world collapsed because I had the opportunity to go to the WHA for a lot of money and I didn't take it – $500,000 a year for 10 years and I didn't take it to stay in Boston."

In New York, Esposito notched career goals No. 600 and 700. He was also part of Canada's 1972 Summit Series team. With 717 career goals (fifth all-time) and 1,590 points (10th all-time), Esposito became the first high-scoring power forward of the Modern Era and was inducted to the Hall of Fame in 1984.

6. Stan Mikita, 1959-1980 – Chicago

Talk to Stan Mikita about the game he loves and you can hear the pride dripping from each sentence.

"I fully intend to shoot 70 when I'm 70," Mikita said on the eve of his 70th birthday in May of 2010. "I shot a 68 when I was 69 last year and even got a hole-in-one that round. It was my 16th career hole-in-one."

Evidently the golf gods have been kind to Mikita as well. Prior to that, the hockey gods had a terrific time creating a player who was part playmaker, part sniper, part antagonist. Mikita moved to St. Catharines, Ont., from Czechoslovakia as a youth and developed an instant chip on his shoulder because of comments he received from other boys at school. In his first seven NHL seasons, he averaged more than 100 penalty minutes, yet also led the league in scoring three times.

Then he suddenly transformed himself into a model citizen and won back-to-back Lady Byng Trophies – and two more scoring titles. "Stan was the perfect center to play with all those years," said his sharp-shooting linemate Bobby Hull. "In junior, they had me playing center and Stan on the wing. It's a good thing they switched things around in Chicago or who knows what would've happened."

Mikita was just 20 when the Hawks won the 1961 Stanley Cup before Chicago's 49-year dry spell ended in 2010. Mikita is also credited with being an innovator of the curved stick in the early 1960s.

5. Howie Morenz, 1923-1937 – Chicago, Rangers, Montreal

In his first organized game of hockey, Howie Morenz played in net. The fledgling goaltender promptly gave up 21 goals as a member of the Mitchell Juveniles and decided on a new path in the sport as a center.

"I guess I'm not a goalie after all," Morenz was quoted as saying in a mid-1930s interview reprinted in a 1948 issue of The Hockey News. "I'll take my action hereafter out front and let someone else worry about the nets."

Worry in the nets was exactly what Morenz caused from there on. 'The Stratford Streak' was a three-time Hart Trophy winner who King Clancy once called the greatest player he had ever seen. Speedy and skilled, Morenz often played 45 to 60 minutes a game and didn't flag near the end.

When he won the NHL scoring title in 1927-28, he did so with 51 points in 43 games, 12 points more than runner-up and linemate Aurel Joliat. This was two seasons before forward passes were allowed in the offensive zone.

Widely considered the NHL's first superstar, Morenz dazzled on the ice in Montreal for 12 seasons, with brief stops in Chicago and New York in between. On Jan. 28, 1937, Chicago's Earl Seibert checked Morenz into the boards. He sustained a badly broken leg and later died in hospital. While some maintain his death was due to the despondency in knowing he would never play for the Habs again, his grandson has since acknowledged that a coronary embolism was the culprit and that blood clots had been seen in an X-ray the night before.

4. Mark Messier, 1979-2004 – Edmonton, Vancouver, Rangers

He's the No. 2 point-producer in NHL history and only Gordie Howe has played more games. He was twice voted the league's most outstanding player by his peers, won six Cups and played in 15 All-Star Games, three Canada Cups, a World Cup and Rendez-vous '87.

But ask Mark Messier for his favorite personal moment and he struggles to think of one. "Impossible to say one thing when you play 26 years," he said. "Just making it; first goal, first Stanley Cup, Canada Cup…"

As an Edmonton Oiler, Messier played second fiddle to Wayne Gretzky. After Gretzky was traded to Los Angeles in 1988, Messier assumed the captaincy and pundits assumed the Oilers were done as Cup champs. But Messier led the Oilers to the Cup in 1990, his fifth title.

Messier played larger than his 6-foot-1, 210-pound frame and was never afraid to throw a forearm shiver or get his elbows up in the corners. "It came down to doing what you had

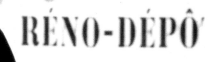

No. 1 | Wayne Gretzky

to do to change the momentum," he said of his physical play. "And you had to make room for yourself on the ice in those days."

And that he did. They've come bigger since, maybe more skilled, maybe with a meaner streak. But no one has put all three together the way Messier did. When you toss in the fact he's widely considered the greatest leader in NHL history, Messier was the total package.

3. Jean Beliveau, 1950-1971 – Montreal

All it took was a gentle squeeze of the elbow by Jean Beliveau. Like everything Beliveau did, it was quiet and understated, but had an enormous effect.

It was the 1971 Stanley Cup final and rookie coach Al MacNeil had benched Montreal Canadiens great Henri Richard. Richard responded by ripping into MacNeil, calling him, "the worst coach I ever played for." But he was just getting warmed up. It was then that Beliveau squeezed his arm and Richard received the message loud and clear: There would be no more spectacular quotes that night.

Beliveau's loyalty to the Canadiens has never been questioned. For 40 years following his 500th goal and leading the Canadiens to his last Stanley Cup as a player, Beliveau was regular at the Bell Centre in Montreal. As former Habs goalie Ken Dryden once put it, Rocket Richard evokes passion, while Beliveau evokes admiration.

As it stands, Beliveau has his name on the Stanley Cup more than any other person – a total of 17 times as a player and executive – and no player in NHL history has his name on the Cup as a captain more times than Beliveau's five.

But it was the class with which Beliveau carried himself that has as much to do with defining him. The Habs are the most revered organization in the game because Beliveau long carried the torch as its most prominent ambassador.

2. Mario Lemieux, 1984-2006 – Pittsburgh

His talents in major junior were god-like; his NHL debut was the confirmation. On his first shift as a member of the Penguins, Mario Lemieux poked the puck away from future Hall of Famer Ray Bourque and dashed down the ice for a breakaway, scoring on a backhand.

After amassing 133 goals and 282 points in 70 games in his final season for the Laval Voisins of the Quebec League, Lemieux jumped to the NHL in 1984-85 and scored 100 points, earning the Calder Trophy.

Though hampered by injuries and a heroic battle with Hodgkin's disease, Lemieux put together one of the greatest NHL careers of all-time. Lemieux captained the Penguins to back-to-back Cups in 1991 and 1992 and was unquestionably The Man in Pittsburgh. He also carries the distinction of scoring five goals in one game in all different manners. On Dec. 31, 1988, Lemieux scored at even strength, on the power play, shorthanded, on a penalty shot and into an empty net.

The cruel fate of Lemieux's career comes in the fact injuries (many were related to his back) and illness limited him to 915 games during 17 seasons (an average of 54 contests per year), with an initial three-season retirement limiting his stat-padding opportunities.

Still, many of his offensive achievements are second only to Wayne Gretzky, though some pros will tell you 'Super Mario' was scarier. "When Mario was on his game, he was the best player I ever played against," Bourque said. "That amount of skill for his size...he was a lot quicker than you would think."

1. Wayne Gretzky, 1979-1999 – Edmonton, Los Angeles, St. Louis, Rangers

Wayne Gretzky earned four Stanley Cup titles. He remains the all-time leading goal-scorer (894) and point-getter (2,857) and will hold those records for years to come...if not forever.

Ten scoring titles bear Gretzky's name. He won nine Hart Trophies. He was awarded the Lady Byng Trophy five times and his two Conn Smythe Trophies attest to his impressive post-season numbers. "I thought he was the smartest player I ever saw," said Hall of Famer Phil Esposito. "Without a doubt. He seemed to know before you what you were going to do with the puck."

Gretzky's competitive nature pushed him to imagine the previously unimaginable on the ice. "I always loved the game enough to enjoy thinking about it quite often," Gretzky once said.

He was also a player whose yearning to succeed outweighed almost all other aspects of his life. "I always knew you had to win at the highest level if you wanted to be seen as a true competitor."

Gretzky and the Oilers won titles in four of five seasons, from 1984 to 1988, until the trade to end all NHL trades took place in the summer of 1988: Gretzky was shipped to Los Angeles.

In his first three years as a King, The Great One scored at least 40 goals and 100 assists. His best hockey in L.A., however, came at the end of 1992-93. In 24 playoff games that year he had 15 goals and 40 points and led the Kings to the Cup final.

That was Gretzky's last Stanley Cup final appearance before he retired in 1999.

MONTREAL
CANADIENS

As you might imagine – and as Habs fans will be sure to quickly point out, no matter how deferential the person they're dealing with – it's a little bit more difficult choosing the 10 best Canadiens of all-time than it is for any other team in history.

So we have to thank The Hockey News senior writer Ken Campbell and his book Habs Heroes: The Greatest Canadiens Ever from 1 to 100, *for our order. Campbell and the experts he consulted listed the top 10 as follows.* **– JG**

Jean Beliveau, Jacques Plante, Toe Blake and Bernie Geoffrion

10. Edouard 'Newsy' Lalonde

The center/rover (Whew! We're going way back here) played 10 years with Montreal from 1912 to 1922, scoring 231 goals in 179 games. Part of just a single Stanley Cup team, he won two Art Ross Trophies and was the top sniper of his time. He was also not afraid to take it to the streets, as his legendary stick-swinging duels with 'Bad' Joe Hall attest to. Hall of Fame: 1950

9. Henri Richard

The center played 20 years with Montreal – the last in 1975 – winning 11 Cups, the most by a player and a ridiculous percentage. 'The Pocket Rocket' was an all-around player who twice led the NHL in assists, but never scored more than 30 goals or 80 points. He finished his career third in Montreal career scoring with 358 goals and 1,046 points in 1,256 games. HoF: 1979

No. 1 | Maurice Richard

8. Patrick Roy

The youngest on our list, Roy arguably had his best days as a member of the Colorado Avalanche. Nevertheless, the goaltender, who some will say (but we won't) is the best ever at his position, played 10 years in Montreal (1985 to 1995) and won two Cups, two Conn Smythe Trophies, three Vezinas, four Jennings' and was a six-time post-season all-star. He is the all-time leader in post-season games played and wins. His work in the 1986 and '93 playoffs is the stuff of legend. HoF: 2006

7. Larry Robinson

Despite being a defenseman, 'Big Bird' is No. 5 on the Habs' career scoring list with 197 goals and 883 points. But he was much more than a finesse player. He was smart, gritty, skilled and tough as nails (his destruction of Philly's Dave 'The Hammer' Schultz in the 1976 Cup final helped lead the Canadiens to four Cups in a row). Robinson played 17 years in Montreal and during the 1970s was the best D-man on arguably the best blueline of all-time on the best team of all-time. HoF: 1995

6. Jacques Plante

So much more than just the innovative goalie who first popularized the mask in the NHL. 'Jake the Snake' was also the first to raise his arm to signify icing, the first to yell directions at retreating teammates, the first to corral pucks and begin breakouts and the first to leave his crease to smother pucks. Oh yeah, he was pretty good, too. With Montreal he won six Vezinas, six Cups (including five in a row in the '50s) one Hart Trophy and was a six-time post-season all-star, all in 10 years with the team. HoF: 1978

5. Howie Morenz

After Newsy Lalonde, the mythical Morenz took the mantle of best Canadiens player. In 12 years with the team he won three Cups, three Harts, two Art Ross Trophies and was a three-time all-star. 'The Stratford Streak' helped the fledgling NHL promote itself with him as its first superstar. Larger than life while alive, Morenz's death only added to his legend. After a particularly brutal hit badly broke his leg in January 1937, Morenz's career was effectively over. He died either of a broken heart or coronary embolism caused by blood clots in his leg. HoF: 1945

4. Guy Lafleur

'Le Demon Blond' did things in the Bleu, Blanc et Rouge that no other Hab did before or after. His 518 goals and 1,246 points place him at the top of Montreal's career scoring list, but he had a stretch in the '70s few can claim to match. From 1974 to 1980, Lafleur averaged 128 points a season, winning three straight Art Ross Trophies and Pearson Awards, two straight Harts (and finishing runner-up the next year) and a Conn Smythe. He also led the league in goals twice during those six seasons. The most dynamic player in team history, he spent 14 seasons with the club from 1971 to 1985. HoF: 1988

3. Doug Harvey

Harvey was a defensive wiz and a brawler when needed, but they broke the offensive-defenseman mold with him and it's he who birthed future stars like Bobby Orr and Paul Coffey. He was the first of his kind and, some will argue, the best blueliner ever. From 1947 to 1961, Harvey was an all-star 10 times, won six Cups and six Norris Trophies (he was a runner-up another time and won it again in 1962 as a Ranger). HoF: 1973

2. Jean Beliveau

'Le Gros Bill' is universally regarded as one of the classiest people to ever grace NHL ice, but he could play some, too. During his 20 years with the Habs he was a 10-time all-star, won 10 Cups, a scoring title and a Conn Smythe. He is, perhaps, the greatest captain the team has ever had – respected and revered by his teammates – and still evokes a sense of awe with his silvery shock of hair and noble demeanor at Canadiens games. HoF: 1972

1. Maurice Richard

'The Rocket' not only led a team, he was a cultural icon in French Canada. Richard could inspire riots as well as Quiet Revolutions and, damn, could he play. The first shooter to score 50 and 500 goals, Richard played with a fire in his belly (and in his eyes). He led the Canadiens' resurgence out of the 1930s and early '40s Cup drought known as the 'Great Darkness' that nearly spelled the end of the franchise altogether. In 18 years with the team he was a 14-time all-star and won eight Cups, retiring as the game's all-time leading goal-scorer. HoF: 1961

WORLD CHAMPIONSHIP
SCORERS

Not surprisingly, former Soviet players dominate the list of World Championship career scorers, just as the USSR dominated the tournament for more than a generation.

From 1954 to 1992, the Soviets won 19 gold medals, including 15 in an 18-tournament span during their heyday.

The Soviet hockey machine was so overwhelming, its traditional rival, Hockey Canada, boycotted international play during parts of the 1970s on the basis the Soviet players were professionals masquerading as amateurs.

There are a many legendary names on this list sprinkled with some stars of yore from outside the USSR. – JG

10. Anatoli Firsov, Soviet Union, 101 points
Firsov played in eight World Championship events, made five all-star teams and led the tournament in scoring in 1967, '68, '69 and '71. His 110 points came in just 62 games.

9. Jiri Holik, Czechoslovakia, 104 points
Uncle to former NHLer Bobby Holik, Jiri Holik leads all players in tournament games played (123) and is tied with two others in A Pool tournaments played (14). He was inducted into the IIHF Hall of Fame in 1999.

8. Veniamin Alexandrov, Soviet Union, 104 points
Inducted into the IIHF Hall of Fame in 2007 (16 years after his death), Alexandrov led the 1966 tournament in scoring with nine goals and 17 points in seven games. The Soviets won silver that year, ending their streak of gold medals at seven.

7. Vladimir Martinec, Czechoslovakia, 110 points
A tournament all-star in 1974, '75, '76 and '77, Martinec is 14th all-time in IIHF games played (289). He was named top forward at the 1976 tournament, when Czechoslovakia won gold and swept the awards.

6. Sergei Makarov, Soviet Union, 118 points
The reason the NHL has a Calder Trophy age limit, Makarov is one of the greatest international performers. He's fifth all-time with 315 IIHF games played and has 11 World Championship medals, including eight gold.

No. 4 | Vladimir Petrov

5. Sven 'Tumba' Johansson, Sweden, 127 points

A hero in Sweden, 'Tumba' was the first great player for the Tre Kroner. He, too, played in 14 World Championships and was twice named the tournament's best forward. 'Tumba' was the first European to attend an NHL training camp when he tried out for Boston in 1957.

4. Vladimir Petrov, Soviet Union, 154 points

The 2006 IIHF Hall inductee also owns 11 medals from the worlds. The center played in the 1972 Summit Series, scoring three goals and seven points in the eight games, while playing an important checking role against the likes of Phil Esposito.

No. 1 | Boris Mikhailov

3. Alexander Maltsev, Soviet Union, 156 points

Another veteran of the Summit Series, Maltsev is third all-time with 12 medals, nine of which were gold, in 12 tournaments. He's also fourth all-time in IIHF games played with 316.

2. Valeri Kharlamov, Soviet Union, 159 points

The legendary Kharlamov just may be the greatest Soviet player to ever hit the ice – so great his ankle was the target of Bobby Clarke's slash in '72, which effectively knocked him out of the Summit Series. Kharlamov was also the highest-scoring Olympian until Teemu Selanne passed him in 2010 in Vancouver. Kharlamov's 105 games at the worlds are tied for eighth all-time; he was a four-time tournament all-star.

1. Boris Mikhailov, Soviet Union, 169 points

Mikhailov captained the Soviets to five gold medals in the '70s and coached Russia to another in 1993. He was twice named top forward, while playing on the USSR's top line with Kharlamov and Petrov. When Mikhailov retired he was carried around the rink on his teammates' shoulders.

40-PLUS NHLERS

Dwayne Roloson recorded four shutouts and a 18-12-4 record in 2010-11 and took his team to the conference final at the tender young age of 41. This past season, a 40-year-old Ray Whitney finished tied for 12th in league scoring and also took his Coyotes to the Final Four.

But are either on of the best NHLers to play into his 40s? The answer is below. – AP

No. 7 | Chris Chelios

10. Teemu Selanne

The 'Finnish Flash' has a handful of impressive records to his name – including most points (37) at the Olympics and single-season goals (76) and points (132) by a rookie – he'll without question be a first-ballot Hall of Famer.

9. Ray Bourque

Bourque's achievements include five Norris Trophies; an NHL-record 13 first-team all-star honors; still-standing records for the most goals, assists and points by a defenseman; and a Stanley Cup with Colorado to cap off his career at age 40. He just turned 51, but Bourque's legacy will last far longer than a half-century.

8. Jacques Plante

Plante was a dominant force on the ice as well, amassing six Stanley Cup championships, a Hart Trophy and seven Vezina Trophies (the last of which he shared as a 40-year-old with Glenn Hall).

7. Chris Chelios

Chelios made his debut with the Montreal Canadiens in 1982-83. In the 26 seasons that followed, he made the playoffs 24 times, won three Norris Trophies and as many Stanley Cups. In his final season, Chelios also played in the American League, becoming the oldest player in that circuit's history. He also is the second-oldest player in NHL history.

6. Steve Yzerman

One of the greatest leaders hockey has ever seen managed to play until age 41 – this, despite suffering brutal injuries that would've retired lesser players far earlier. Three Stanley Cups, a Conn Smythe Trophy and a Selke Trophy don't begin to illustrate how much he meant to the Red Wings; that he captained the team from age 21 until his retirement in 2006 still stands as the record for the longest captaincy in North American pro sports history.

5. Doug Harvey

In 24 pro seasons, Harvey made his name as a creative blueliner who was the game's Bobby Orr before Bobby Orr arrived. He won seven Norris Trophies and six Stanley Cups in the 1940s and '50s, played until he was 44 years old and was ranked No. 6 on THN's list of the 100 Greatest Hockey Players.

4. Terry Sawchuk

Sawchuk played until he was 40 and likely would've played longer were it not for his tragic death at that age. Nevertheless, he won four Cups, as many Vezina Trophies, the Calder Trophy and held the NHL record for career shutouts (103) until Martin Brodeur in broke it in 2009.

3. Mark Messier

Second overall in all-time NHL regular season points, playoff points (295) and regular season games played (1,756), Messier lasted until age 43 before hanging up his skates as a New York Ranger. Like Yzerman, he is renowned for his leadership ability, but six Cups, two Hart Trophies and a Conn Smythe Trophy demonstrate his all-around impact.

2. Nicklas Lidstrom

The humble Lidstrom, who turned 42 in April, probably wouldn't like to be known as a living legend. Yet with every passing season his superb skill level failed to fall off, that label fit perfectly. His four Stanley Cups, seven Norris Trophies (the last of which came when he was 41), 10 appearances as a first-team all-star (plus two more as a second-teamer) and all-around consistent play prove he's one of the best blueliners ever to grace an NHL rink.

1. Gordie Howe

By almost anyone's estimation, Howe is one of the three best NHLers of all-time. His accomplishments are too numerous to detail here, but the simple fact he was able to continue playing through his 40s and all the way to age 51 is a feat that likely never will be matched. THN

No. 1 | Gordie Howe

SUTTERS

They are, without a doubt, hockey's royal family. And like most reigning monarchs, they've been through their fair share of bloodbaths. Whether it was against each other on the frozen slough in Viking or against the best the NHL had to offer, the Sutters have always picked (and finished) their own battles.

And they've been pretty good hockey players along the way, too. Here are our top 10 Sutters, with a pair of unrelated namesakes rounding out list. **– Ken Campbell**

Duane, Rich, Louis, Ron and Brent Sutter

10. Fabian Sutter

We thought we'd throw a little curve at you with No. 10 on the list. You may have never heard of Fabian Sutter, but hockey fans in Switzerland certainly have. Sutter represented his country in the World Under-18 championship in 2000 and the world juniors in 2001 and 2002. He just completed his 13th season in the Swiss League, where he won championships with Davos in 2002 and 2005.

9. Rich Sutter

A former scout for the 2012 Western Conference finalist Phoenix Coyotes, Rich played 13 years in the NHL and maxed out at 20 goals and 42 points with the Vancouver Canucks in 1986-87. With 1,411 career penalty minutes, he's the second-most penalized player of the Sutter clan.

8. Brandon Sutter
By far the most accomplished of the second-generation Sutters thus far, the son of Brent has already played almost 300 games in the NHL for the Carolina Hurricanes and remains a bright spot in the organization. In international play, he helped Canada win the 2008 World Junior Championship.

7. Patrick Sutter
Anybody who can play defense at 5-foot-8 and 171 pounds is tough enough to be a Sutter in our book. One of the top non-NHL defensemen Switzerland has ever produced, Patrick has played in seven World Championships and one Olympic Games for Switzerland. He won two Swiss League championships and was the league's top defenseman in 1999-2000.

6. Ron Sutter
The last of the Sutter brothers to retire, Ron was an industrious defensive center for most of his 18-year career, but did have some very productive seasons early on when he played for the Philadelphia Flyers along with his twin brother Rich. He and Rich are believed to be the only players in NHL history to have their first and last names on the backs of their sweaters. Now the director of player development for the Calgary Flames, Ron won a Memorial Cup with the Lethbridge Broncos in 1983. He was also the highest drafted of the Sutters, going fourth overall in 1982.

5. Darryl Sutter
He had the shortest playing career and is the lowest scoring of the original six Sutters, but Darryl gets high marks for his coaching career. An integral part of the Los Angeles Kings' Stanley Cup championship in 2012, Sutter has coached more than 900 games in the NHL. He also led the Indianapolis Ice to a Turner Cup (emblematic of supremacy in the defunct International League) and helmed the Calgary Flames to a Cup final in 2004.

4. Brian Sutter
The oldest of the Sutter clan and the only one to have his number retired by an organization, Brian served as captain of the St. Louis Blues for nine years and was named coach of the team almost immediately after he retired. With 1,786 penalty minutes in 779 games, he's also the most penalized of the Sutters. He never won a Stanley Cup as a player or coach, but won the Jack Adams Award in 1991 and guided the senior AAA Bentley Generals to the Allan Cup in 2009.

3. Duane Sutter
The most decorated of the Sutter clan, Duane won Stanley Cups in each of his first four NHL seasons as a member of the New York Islanders. Tough, but skilled, he led all Islanders with seven points in the 1983 Stanley Cup final against the Edmonton Oilers. He is now a pro scout for the Oilers.

2. Brent Sutter

The most talented and productive of all the Sutters, Brent won two Stanley Cups alongside Duane with the Islanders and was a mainstay for Canada in the Canada Cup, winning the tournament three times during his career. After retiring from the NHL in 1998, he bought the Red Deer Rebels and led them to the Memorial Cup in 2001. He was also behind the bench for back-to-back gold medals for Canada in the 2005 and '06 World Junior Championships.

1. Grace and Louis Sutter (With a shout-out to Gary)

None of the Sutters would be in the NHL today if not for Grace and Louis, who raised seven boys on a farm in Viking, Alta., southeast of Edmonton. They went on to see six of their seven boys play in the NHL, with the exception of Gary, their oldest, who turned down a chance to play major junior hockey. But Gary taught all his brothers how to skate and the ones who played in the NHL maintained that Gary was the most talented, and best skater, of them all. THN

No. 2 | Brent Sutter

GAME 7
PERFORMANCES

As kids, with our plastic blades on neighborhood streets or mini-sticks in hotel hallways, we don't dream of scoring a series-winner in Games 4, 5 or 6...no, we always imagine ourselves in the one-game-takes-it-all showdown, having the game of our lives.

Which players got to live out their dreams over the years? Let's look at the league's 10 best Game 7 performances and find out. **– JG**

No. 10 | Jeremy Roenick

10. Jeremy Roenick, San Jose, 2008

One of the last, best moments of Roenick's standout career came when he was a San Jose Shark taking on Calgary in the quarterfinal. Roenick was a healthy scratch in Game 6, but answered his critics in the best possible way - with a two-goal, four-point effort to eliminate the Flames in a 5-3 win.

9. Alex Delvecchio, Detroit, 1955

The Red Wings legend and his teammates faced a tough challenge in the Stanley Cup final against the Montreal Canadiens, but Delvecchio scored Detroit's first and last goals and assisted on the other in a 3-1 victory.

8. Ruslan Fedotenko, Tampa Bay, 2004

The undrafted Fedotenko didn't get the hype or accolades Lightning teammates Vincent Lecavalier and Martin St-Louis received, but he did score both Bolts goals in Tampa's 2-1 Cup-claiming victory.

No. 1 | Wayne Gretzky

7. Kelly Hrudey, Islanders, 1987

Now a *Hockey Night In Canada* analyst, Hrudey was goaltending for the Isles nearly a quarter-century ago in the then-Patrick Division semifinal when he was bombarded by 75 shots from the Washington Capitals in a quadruple overtime game that turned out to be the sixth-longest in league history. Hrudey stopped all but two of those shots in New York's 3-2 win.

6. Turk Broda, Toronto, 1942

The goaltending icon starred for Toronto on a number of occasions, but never looked better than when he led the Leafs to an improbable series comeback from a 3-0 deficit. In the deciding Game 7, Broda surrendered the first goal to the Wings, but protected the net perfectly after that in a 3-1 win before a delirious crowd at Maple Leaf Gardens.

5. Henri Richard, Montreal, 1971

Known as 'The Pocket Rocket,' Richard was prominent in Montreal's come-from-behind Game 7 win against Chicago in the Cup final. The Hawks were up 2-0 in the second period when Canadiens forward Jacques Lemaire scored from outside the blueline to cut the lead in half. Richard scored the next two goals to give the Habs the win.

4. Curtis Joseph, Edmonton, 1997

Joseph and the Oilers went into enemy territory in Dallas for Game 7 of their first round series – and the goalie known as 'Cujo' stopped 38 of 41 shots as Edmonton won 4-3 in overtime.

3. Mark Messier, Rangers, 1994

The Rangers captain famously guaranteed a win against New Jersey in the Eastern Conference final, then followed that up with the Stanley Cup-winning goal in Game 7 against Vancouver.

2. Ron Hextall, Philadelphia, 1987

It's rare to see the Conn Smythe Trophy given to a member of the losing team, but that's what happened to Hextall in Philly's Cup final series loss to the Oilers. Hextall made 40 saves in a losing cause in the Flyers' Game 7, 3-1 loss and was spectacular throughout the series.

1. Wayne Gretzky, Los Angeles, 1993

During the Campbell Conference final between Toronto and the Kings, Gretzky put up arguably the best single-game showing of his unrivaled career, recording a hat trick and virtually willing L.A. to victory over a plucky, Doug Gilmour-led Leafs squad. ▄▄▄

THINGS THAT
CHANGED THE GAME

There are many innovations and additions that have shaped the league we know and love (most of the time). For example, 2012 marks the 60th anniversary of when the Canadian Broadcasting Corporation began televising NHL games, forever changing the relationship between fans and their franchises. It's also the 120th anniversary of the Stanley Cup being donated by Lord Stanley of Preston, the Governor General of Canada at the time, to the Ottawa Hockey Club. It was originally called the Dominion Hockey Challenge Cup and was meant as an award for the best amateur ice hockey team in Canada. But not even these made the cut.

From the introduction of the six-man game in 1911, to the unification of the WHA and the NHL in 1979, these top 10 things in hockey history have made the game what it is today. – **JG**

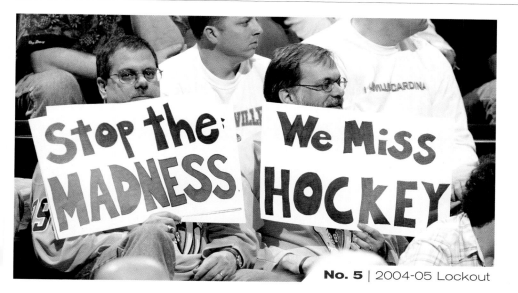

No. 5 | 2004-05 Lockout

10. The elimination of the rover and the introduction of forward pass

The six-player game was born when the rover was eliminated in 1911, formalizing the five skater positions and the goaltender. Gameplay as we know it began with the institution of the forward pass in all three zones in 1929. Forward passing was just that, players were allowed to pass the puck ahead. It led to the offside rule and greatly enhanced offense – goal totals more than doubled in the first year of the rule. Without these two innovations, hockey would be an entirely different sport.

No. 1 | The Entry Draft

9. The Summit Series

The eight-game marathon between Canada and the Soviet Union in 1972 became a microcosm for the Cold War and East vs. West geopolitics. For hockey it showcased European strategy and talent and united Canada hockey-wise for the first time. Anglo-French bi-partisanship remains to this day, but the idea that maybe Canadians weren't far-and-away the best on ice brought the two groups closer than they had ever been.

8. The Miracle on Ice

The U.S. victory at the 1980 Winter Olympics in Lake Placid was to Americans what the Summit Series was to Canadians. Besting the powerhouse Soviets and then Finland for the gold medal remains the biggest moment in USA Hockey history and awoke a nation to the game.

7. The World Hockey Association

The WHA changed the world of hockey forever during its seven-year run: Challenging the NHL's monopoly with bigger paychecks and ground-breaking contracts to the likes of Bobby Hull; bringing Europeans and their style of play to North America; signing 17-year-olds, which basically forced the 18-year-old draft into existence; and playing big-time hockey in the Sun Belt. The WHA made hockey fun again and changed the way the NHL conducted business.

6. Wayne Gretzky

Whether it was making his professional debut at 17, amassing goal, assist and point totals never before conceived of, his trade from Edmonton to Los Angeles – which broke the hearts of Oilers fans and Canadians in general – or even his role in the Phoenix Coyotes debacle, Gretzky has been at the center of important events in the evolution of hockey on and off the ice for more than 30 years.

5. The 2004-05 lockout

The lockout single-handedly altered the face of the NHL. The economics of the game were drastically changed, in both the way franchises worked together and how they worked with the players, the salary cap was instituted and the on-ice game was changed with the elimination of the red line and a new standard for enforcing rules.

4. The NHLPA

The formation and growth of the NHL Players' Association changed the face of the NHL. Players didn't always share agents and information, collectively bargain or even socialize with one another unless they were teammates. Before the NHLPA was created in 1957, players were basically chattel, subject to the whims of owners and without any means to stand up and have their grievances heard or affect change in any way.

3. Expansion

The first round of expansion in 1967 suddenly created twice as many NHL jobs for players who had previously languished in the minors and exposed the western part of the continent to the NHL product. Expansion has been hit-and-miss, with success stories, but also a watered-down product, a southern footprint scarred by failed and failing franchises and an alienated Canadian fan base. Still, for all its faults, expansion's importance can't be argued.

2. Europeans

Beginning with the Summit Series, continuing with the WHA and NHL pioneers such as Inge Hammarstrom and Borje Salming in the 1970s, the Stastny brothers' defections and the brilliance of Jari Kurri in the '80s, and finally the *en masse* arrival of Eastern Bloc players in the '90s, hockey is better thanks to the mingling of the European and North American styles. And Europeans saved the NHL. Without them there simply wouldn't have been, and still wouldn't be, enough top-end talent to sustain the league's aggressive expansion.

1. The entry draft

Prior to 1963, the Original Six teams scoured Canada and the hockey hotbeds in the U.S. for teenaged talent and "sponsored" the amateur teams they liked best. That sponsorship gave them exclusive rights to players from those teams, basically making them property for life. What's more, teams had territorial rights – the Canadiens had first dibs on all Quebec-born players, for instance. It all began to end in 1963 with the institution of the Amateur Draft of un-sponsored players. What is now the annual NHL draft has gone through a number of evolutions the past 46 years. Nothing else has changed the face of the NHL quite like the way players are distributed. Teams still must draft well to ensure success, but at least everyone has a fighting chance. THN

SINGLE-SEASON
ASSIST TOTALS

Behind every great goal-scorer are players that know how to set up a shot. The goal-scorers tend to get most of the glory, but save for the breakaways, where would they be without that perfect pass?

Based on numbers, Wayne Gretzky would take nine out of the 10 spots on a list of single-season assist leaders. Instead, we decided that players can only appear once. Take a wild guess at who grabbed No. 1. – JG

No. 7 | Pat LaFontaine

10. Paul Coffey, Edmonton, 90 assists, 1985-86

The second-highest scoring defenseman in NHL history makes the list here over Steve Yzerman's 90 helpers in 1988-89 on the back of playing one less game (79 versus 80). The total is the 26th most in league history. Coffey was one of four Oilers to top the 100-point mark that season; Gretzky set a record with 215.

9. Ron Francis, Pittsburgh, 92 assists, 1995-96

The fourth-highest scoring player in NHL history joined the vaunted Penguins offense of the '90s from Hartford and flourished for seven-plus seasons. His 92 assists are the 21st-most in league history and 16 more than his next-highest total.

8. Peter Stastny, Quebec, 93 assists, 1981-82

Stastny was a 25-year-old NHL sophomore when he posted the most assists ever by a European player. He was one of three Stastny brothers on the Nordiques that season and Marian and Anton weren't too shabby, either.

7. Pat LaFontaine, Buffalo, 95 assists, 1992-93

The most helpers ever by a U.S.-born player also represents the 17th-most in league history. LaFontaine's gaudy total came courtesy of his sublime skill, but also Alex Mogilny's 76-goal campaign.

6. Doug Gilmour, Toronto, 95 assists, 1992-93

'Killer' gets the nod over LaFontaine for playing one fewer game. Gilmour won the Selke Trophy for his work that year, which included 127 points and a plus-32 rating.

5. Joe Thornton, Boston-San Jose, 96 assists, 2005-06

The only active player to make the list, Jumbo Joe's total comes in at No. 16 overall. Amazingly, Thornton was traded that season. He tallied 24 assists in 23 games with the Bruins then burst out with 72 helpers in 58 contests with the Sharks.

4. Adam Oates, Boston, 97 assists, 1992-93

Oates led the Bruins in goals (45) and assists in the 'Year of the Helper' and had 40 more points than any other Bruin. He finished third in league scoring behind Mario Lemieux and LaFontaine.

3. Bobby Orr, Boston, 102 assists, 1970-71

The most prolific-scoring blueliner in hockey and some argue the best player in history is one of just three players to crack the 100-assist mark. Orr won his second of three consecutive Hart Trophies that year and the fourth of eight consecutive Norris Trophies.

2. Mario Lemieux, Pittsburgh, 114 assists, 1988-89

His 114 helpers rank No. 2 here, but just eighth overall. Lemieux finished with a career-best 199 points that season to win his second of six Art Ross Trophies.

1. Wayne Gretzky, Edmonton, 163 assists, 1985-86

Yes, he has nine of 10, but he's also got 11 of 12 of the highest assist totals in league history. He had more career regular season assists than any other player has had total points and 74 more playoff assists than No. 2 on the list. Gretzky reached assist and point totals that had never been imagined before and will never be seen again. He is the greatest set-up man in hockey history. ◼THN◼

No. 2 | Mario Lemieux

FEMALE PLAYERS

Women's hockey has made quantum leaps in quality and popularity in recent decades, making the task of choosing the 10 all-time best female players even more difficult. So with a nod to early pioneers of the women's game such as Hilda Ranscombe, here are the top 10 female players of the modern era. **– AP**

No. 7 | Kim St-Pierre

10. Cassie Campbell

She didn't have the high-end scoring talent of most of the women on this list, but Campbell captained the Canadian National Women's team from 2001 until she retired in 2006 – the longest-serving captaincy in Canadian hockey history – and Team Canada was 129-26-2 when she was in the lineup. She is also the only captain of either sex to lead Canada to two Olympic gold medals.

9. Angela Ruggiero

In her 13-year career that ended in 2011, Ruggiero was a big, tough defenseman who earned each of the many accolades she received, including THN's Best Female Player Award in 2003. An Olympic gold medalist in 1998, the Simi Valley, Calif., native was the first female player to play in a North American men's pro game on January 28, 2005, when she and her brother Bill, played for the Central League's Tulsa Oilers.

8. Kim Martin

The Swedish netminder first burst on the hockey scene when she starred for her national team at the IIHF's 2001 World Championship. She was just fifteen at the time. Since then, Martin backstopped her countrywomen to an Olympic bronze medal in 2002 and a silver in 2006, when she and Sweden upset the heavily favored Americans in the semi-final – the first time either the USA or Canada lost to any third nation in international play.

7. Kim St-Pierre

The Canadian goaltender won Olympic gold medals in 2002 – when she was also named best goalie in the tournament – 2006 and 2010 and was the first woman in Canadian college sports history to win a men's regular season game. St-Pierre also has five world championship golds.

6. Jayna Hefford

Hefford has enjoyed a superb career as one of the women's game's most dangerous snipers and scored the gold-medal-winning goal for Canada at the 2002 Olympics. The Kingston, Ont., native has three Olympic gold medals to her credit and seven World Championship gold medals.

5. Riikka Nieminen

The greatest European female player of all time, Nieminen scored 109 goals and 204 points in 118 games for Finland and was the top point-getter at the 1998 Olympic Games – where the Finns won the bronze – with seven goals and 12 points in six games. She is one of only four women (including Angela James, Geraldine Heaney and Cammi Granato) to be inducted into the IIHF Hall of Fame.

4. Cammi Granato

The best-ever American women's player, Granato captained the 1998 gold-medal winning Olympic team and scored the first-ever Olympic goal in U.S women's history. The Illinois native was the first of two women (the other was Angela James) inducted into the Hockey Hall of Fame in 2010.

3. Geraldine Heaney

She was born in Belfast, Ireland, but Heaney was raised in Toronto and became the greatest defenseman in women's hockey history. She won seven World Championships – and was named top defenseman at that tournament on two occasions – as well as two Olympic medals: gold in Salt Lake and silver in Nagano.

2. Hayley Wickenheiser

A child prodigy who made Team Canada at age 15 and has starred ever since, Wickenheiser has been the dominant player of her generation. Besides her three Olympic gold medals and seven World championship gold medals, she is a pioneer, having been the first female player to score a goal in a professional men's league game when she played in Finland in 2003.

1. Angela James

Often called "the Wayne Gretzky of women's hockey," James grew up in Toronto and set the bar for the first generation of modern female players. In the inaugural World Championship in 1990, she had 11 goals in five games and went on to win four World Championship gold medals while scoring 26 goals and 46 points in 35 career games representing Canada in international play. ▥

No. 1 | Angela James

DETROIT RED WINGS

There is no such thing as a dynasty in the modern-day NHL, but the Detroit Red Wings come about as close to that status as anyone in the league.

Oh, what they heck, they're a dynasty. Perhaps not quite on par with the team that won four Stanley Cups in six years in the 1950s, but any team that can have their kind of record for sustained excellence in today's NHL is allowed to be the one ther changes the definition.

And it's from these two generations that all of the Red Wings top 10 players of all-time are culled. Certainly more than any other Original Six team, the Red Wings have a larger dose of modern-day players among their pantheon of greats. **– KC**

No. 7 | Pavel Datsyuk

10. Alex Delvecchio

It wasn't just that Delvecchio played at a high level, it's that he did so being one of the cleanest players in the history of the game. The center won three Lady Byng Trophies and never had more than 37 penalty minutes in a single season. Another player overshadowed by the giant presence of Gordie Howe, Delvecchio played 24 seasons with the Red Wings and won three Stanley Cups. Hall of Fame: 1977

9. Sid Abel

Always overshadowed by his 'Production Line' mates, Abel was an outstanding set-up man for Howe and Ted Lindsay for five seasons during the trio's glory years. He managed to win the Hart Trophy in 1949 and was a first-time all-star at center twice. HoF: 1969

8. Sergei Fedorov

Fedorov, who could play all three forward positions and even played some on the blueline, could certainly be mercurial and a tease with his talent at times, but there is little doubt he was one of the most dynamic players of the 1990s. A constant two-way threat, Fedorov is the only player in NHL history to win the Hart and Selke Trophies in the same season, which he did in 1993-94. He followed that up with a Selke in 1996. In the four playoff seasons between 1995 and 1998, he averaged 21 points.

7. Pavel Datsyuk

On a franchise that has had an embarrassment of riches when it comes to two-way players, Datsyuk is the greatest of them all. There are those who play with him who claim the center would be a top-three scorer every season if he did not take so much pride in his defensive game. Any conversation of the best player in the world right now has to have Datsyuk's name in it.

6. Terry Sawchuk

Considered by many, including THN, to be the greatest goalie of all-time, Sawchuk was a brilliant, but tragic figure who died at age 40 after an injury-filled career. He led the Red Wings to three Stanley Cups in the 1950s and won three Vezina Trophies in the span of four seasons. Five straight seasons he had a goals-against average under 2.00 and in 1952 recorded four playoff shutouts in just eight games as the Red Wings swept both series en route to the Stanley Cup. HoF: 1971

5. Red Kelly

His eight Stanley Cups, four of them with the Red Wings and four with the Maple Leafs, make Kelly the most-decorated player to never play for the Montreal Canadiens. Kelly was also the first winner of the Norris Trophy and the last defenseman before Brian Campbell in 2012 to win the Lady Byng Trophy, something he did three times with the Red Wings. HoF: 1969

4. Ted Lindsay

When Lindsay retired in 1965, he did so as the NHL's all-time leader in penalty minutes, despite the fact he topped out at 5-foot-8 and 160 pounds. More importantly, he was also the league's highest-scoring left winger and one of the most singularly focused players in the history of the game. He is also the only player to lead the league in goals (1947-48), assists (1949-50), points ('49-50) and penalty minutes (1959-60). All but the last were accomplished with the Red Wings. HoF: 1966

3. Nicklas Lidstrom

He is without question the greatest European player of all-time, the best defenseman the Red Wings have ever produced and has recently entered the discussion as the second-greatest defenseman of all-time. Lidstrom's game was always one based on efficiency and smarts, which was the main reason for his sustained level of excellence.

2. Steve Yzerman

'Stevie Y' was one of the most dynamic offensive players of his era before morphing into one of the greatest two-way players and leaders the game has ever seen. Playing largely in the shadow of Wayne Gretzky and Mario Lemieux, the pivot had five 50-goal seasons and six consecutive 100-point seasons before leading the Red Wings to four Stanley Cups. HoF: 2009

1. Gordie Howe

To give you an idea how good Howe was for how long, consider this: the right winger scored more goals after his 30th birthday than before it and he scored a mind-boggling 44 goals at the age of 41. Six Hart Trophies and as many scoring championships mark his crowning individual achievements, but it was his longevity that defined him. Oh yes, and Howe was one of the most vicious players of his era. HoF: 1972

No. 1 | Gordie Howe

SINGLE-GAME
PLAYOFF SCORERS

A lot of complaints emerged – especially during the playoffs – about the drop in scoring across the NHL in 2010-12. No one was complaining during the Flyers-Penguins Round 1 goal-fest, however, when the series averaged 9.3 goals per game and produced one of the Top 10 most productive performances in playoff history.

Only 14 players have had six or more points in a post-season game (Patrik Elias, with two goals and four assists, Geoff Courtnall and Paul Coffey with a goal and five assists and Mikko Leinonen with six helpers didn't make our cut). Not surprisingly, Wayne Gretzky and Mario Lemieux did it more than once, so we only included them a single time on the list. *– AP*

No. 8 | Claude Giroux

10. John Anderson, Hartford – April 12, 1986

In the Whalers' 9-4 win over Quebec, Anderson, who after 12 years playing in the NHL has had successful coaching career, posted two goals and four assists.

No. 1 | Mario Lemieux

9. Dickie Moore, Montreal – March 25, 1954

The Hall of Famer had six points – a pair of goals and four helpers – in the Canadiens' 8-1 demolishing of Boston.

8. Claude Giroux, Philadelphia – April 13, 2012

Bobby Clarke may have had a brain cramp at the podium on the day the Flyers drafted him, but everyone knew Giroux's name after he put up three of each in an 8-5 victory over rival Pittsburgh.

7. Guy Lafleur, Montreal – April 11, 1977

'The Flower' was never more dangerous in the playoffs than the night he had a hat trick of goals and assists to power the Canadiens to
a 7-2 win over St. Louis.

6. Johan Franzen, Detroit – May 6, 2010

One of the most dangerous current Wings players, Franzen had four goals and two assists in Detroit's 7-1 win over San Jose.

5. Phil Esposito, Boston – April 2, 1969

Esposito was just 27 when he notched four goals and six points to help the Bruins to a 10-0 shellacking of Toronto.

4. Darryl Sittler, Toronto – April 22, 1976

Sittler, who holds the record for points in a regular season game (10), had a whopping five goals and six points in the Leafs' 8-5 win over Philly.

3. Wayne Gretzky, Edmonton – April 17, 1983

Playing against the Calgary Flames, The Great One exploded for four goals and three assists in the Oilers' 10-2 victory. Gretzky had two other seven-point playoff games in his career and is the only NHLer in history to have finished with seven in a single game. He's also one of only two players, along with Leinonen, to have six assists in a playoff game.

2. Patrick Sundstrom, New Jersey – April 22, 1988

In the Devils' 10-4 rout of the Washington Capitals, Sundstrom registered a hat trick while also chipping in with five assists for eight points.

1. Mario Lemieux, Pittsburgh – April 25, 1989

One of the greatest players in league history, Lemieux posted an eight-point night with five goals and three assists in a wild 10-7 shootout against the Flyers.

TEENAGE PLAYERS

Legendary humorist and writer Erma Bombeck once wrote, "Never lend your car to anyone to whom you have given birth." That's another way of saying that regardless of the generation, teenagers are perpetually pretty much going to hell in a handcart.

Well, from among this bunch of louts we've been able to identify a few of them who turned out just fine. It's not often that teenaged players turn in classic performances in the NHL, but there are enough of them that we had a little trouble trimming the list to the 10 best.

Here are the top 10 NHL seasons by teenagers, keeping in mind that the player had to be a teenager for the majority of the season in question. – KC

No. 6 | Dale Hawerchuk

10. Bep Guidolin

When Guidolin played his first NHL game for the Boston Bruins Nov. 12, 1942, he established a mark that will almost certainly never be broken, since he was just 16 years and 11 months old at the time. Little known fact: his linemate for the Bruins was a 17-year-old named Don Gallinger.

9. Bryan Trottier

In the first season of his Hall of Fame career, the 19-year-old Trottier scored 32 goals and 95 points for the New York Islanders in 1975-76. It stood as the NHL record for assists by a rookie until Peter Stastny broke the mark five years later at the age of 24.

8. Mario Lemieux

Three minutes into his first NHL game, which was played six days after his 19th birthday, Lemieux stripped Ray Bourque of the puck and scored. He scored 42 more times and totalled 100 points for a woeful Pittsburgh Penguins team in 1984-85 and won the Calder Trophy.

7. Larry Murphy

The 60 assists and 76 points Murphy scored for the Los Angeles Kings in 1980-81 established rookie records for defensemen that still stand today. Even though he turned 20 that season, it wasn't until March, 1981 so he played almost all of the season as a 19-year-old.

6. Dale Hawerchuk

An 18-year-old for all but the very last day of the regular season in 1981-82, Hawerchuk took the NHL by storm with 45 goals and 103 points for the Winnipeg Jets and won the Calder Trophy over 20-year-old Barry Pedersen.

5. Jimmy Carson

After scoring 79 points as a rookie for the Los Angeles Kings, Carson exploded for 55 goals and 107 points as a 19-year-old in 1987-88. His reward for the feat? That summer he was traded to the Edmonton Oilers in the Wayne Gretzky blockbuster.

4. Sidney Crosby

Following up his 102-point rookie season, Crosby scored 36 goals and 120 points in 2006-07 for the Pittsburgh Penguins and, at the age of 19, became the youngest player in NHL history to win a scoring championship. He also won his first Hart Trophy that season.

3. Bobby Orr

Bobby Orr's rookie numbers are not eye-popping when you compare them to the totals that came later in his career, but his 13 goals and 41 points were impressive enough to net him the Calder Trophy in 1966-67 at the age of 18. He was a second-team all-star as well, then went on to be named a first-teamer eight straight times.

2. Wayne Gretzky

A 137-point season might not seem terribly impressive when you stack it up against the prodigious numbers Wayne Gretzky produced in the seasons after, but he posted 51-86-137 totals in his first season (1979-80). He couldn't win the Calder because he had already played in the World Hockey Association and missed out on the Art Ross because Marcel Dionne scored more goals, so he had to settle for the Hart and Lady Byng Trophies, all before he turned 20.

1. Tom Barrasso

You might take issue with this choice, but consider that Barrasso won both the Calder and Vezina Trophies in 1984, one year after playing high school hockey in Massachusetts. Barrasso compiled a 26-12-3 record that season as an 18-19 year old and was named a first-team all-star for the only time in his career. ▣

No. 1 | Tom Barrasso

SUPERSTITIONS

If there's one thread that binds all sports together, it's superstitions. Jumping over the chalk base line while leaving the field, dribbling the ball a specific number of times at the free throw line, repeating a pre-shot routine on the golf course, holding hands with youngsters as you head onto the pitch, taping your ankles or fingers just so before kickoff, whatever.

All have their place in their games' lore. With that in mind, he's a guide to hockey's best superstitions. Just don't step on the logo. – JG

No. 10 | Jason Spezza

10. Tape two

As the most important instrument in all of hockeydom, the stick has been doctored and babied for decades. With the coming of composite sticks, the doctoring has slowed. But players still insist on taping their sticks in a specific manner.

9. The cookie toss

Glenn Hall is one of the NHL's all-time greatest goalies: 502 consecutive games in an era before goalie masks were the norm, three Vezina Trophies, 407 wins. But Hall vomited before every game and believed he'd lose if didn't.

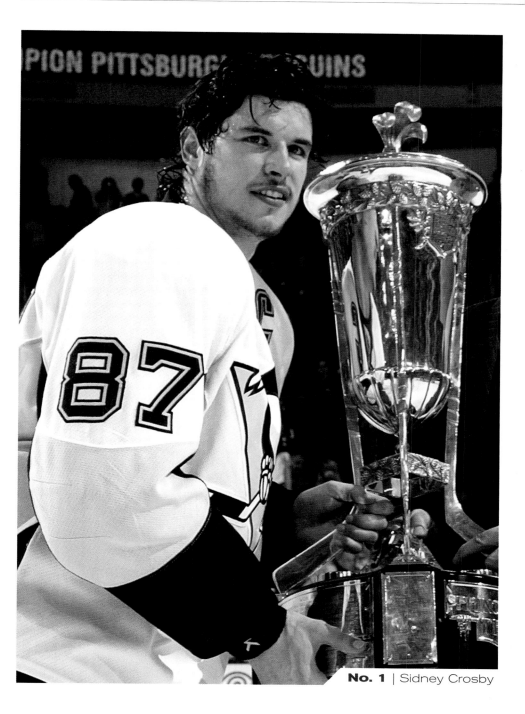

No. 1 | Sidney Crosby

8. The march

On every team, there's an order to which players leave the dressing room for the ice. Whether it's the captain first, the starting goalie last or a veteran tapping each player with his stick, it happens the same way every game.

7. Gearing up

Many players have their own rhyme and reason for the seemingly random practice to putting on their equipment. Do it just so or start all over.

6. One final stop

The legendary Ken Dryden would never leave the net during warmup until he had made one final save. But playing for the powerhouse Canadiens in the 1970s meant that was not always easy. Larry Robinson picked up on it and took to making sure Dryden had an easy one to stop if the goalie was having problems. But Dryden figured Robinson out and began to work even harder to make that final save before Robinson lobbed an easy one his way.

5. OK, but it'll cost you a buck

At the 2002 Salt Lake Olympics, Canada won men's hockey gold for the first time since 1952. And at center ice was buried a Canadian one-dollar coin. Burying a 'loonie' at center ice for international competitions has since become a superstition, albeit one other countries are not overly enthralled with.

4. The tobacco toss

In no way are we advocating smoking – not that you could now in most arenas, anyway – but there were few more masculine-looking superstitions than Stan Mikita tossing his cigarette over his left shoulder as he exited the tunnel for the ice at the old Chicago Stadium.

3. Conversing with iron

Goalies are weird. Period. And Patrick Roy is one of the weirdest in recent memory. He had a number of superstitions, including carrying on running conversations with every goalie's best on-ice friends, the goal posts.

2. Grow baby, grow

It's believed the Islanders began the playoff beard superstition during their Stanley Cup run in the 1980s. It worked, too. They won four Cups in four years, the last in 1983.

1. Don't touch that

There's only one trophy teams want and to touch the Clarence Campbell or Prince of Wales Trophy en route to the Stanley Cup is anathema right? Well, not exactly. Since 2001 teams that grab the conference bauble are just 4-5 in the final. ᴛʜɴ

JEREMY ROENICK
QUOTES

Over his 20-year career Jeremy Roenick was known as one of the NHL's most quotable players. He was entertaining, controversial and never afraid to speak his mind, which is a refreshing character trait in this day and age of media-trained, cliché-machine sports figures. Here are our favorites of his many classic quotes. – JG

10. "A lot of kids are 'We lose, I'm still gonna drive away in my Mercedes.' How are they gonna throw themselves in front of a slapshot or take a punch in the mouth to get in front of the net and score a goal? When this team gets in trouble, we have no emotion. So I've gotta attack "em."

– On teaching the younger San Jose Sharks that losing just isn't acceptable.

9. "When we watch hockey games and see 8,000 fans in D.C., you cringe as a player...Those cities that aren't pulling their weight in terms of drawing fans and revenue are hurting everybody as a whole, not just that city."

– On the state of some NHL markets prior to the lockout (and, obviously, prior to Alex Ovechkin's arrival in Washington).

8. "They just love to complain about me because I'm an American who gets more press than their Canadian players."

– On his love/hate relationship with the Canadian media.

7. "The coach just doesn't like him for some ungodly-known reason. I think he's got a grudge against American players, but he does not like 'Cheli' at all...If you'd know some of the things that Babcock says to Chris Chelios, it would make your stomach churn."

– On Chris Chelios' lack of playing time during the 2009 playoffs.

6. "We did not lose to a bunch of scrubs. We lost to the best players in the world, bar none. And you could tell they needed it. It seemed like 50 years of emotion was pent up because they were flying out there."

– On Team USA's loss to Canada in the gold medal game at the 2002 Olympics.

5. "When they saw that 12 percent out of the paycheck, the guys on our team were bitching and moaning and complaining about it...This is after we already had given back 24 percent and taken a ($39-million) salary cap."

– On NHL salary escrow after the lockout and the seeming lack of understanding players had about the economics of the new NHL.

4. "I liked Patrick's quote, (that) he would have stopped me. I wanted to know where he was in Game 3. He was probably getting his jock out of the rafters of the United Center."
– On Patrick Roy after Game 4 of the conference semifinal between Chicago and Coloradoin 1996. (Roy's retort: "I can't really hear what Jeremy says, because I've got my two Stanley Cup rings plugging my ears.")

3. "Because wives and girlfriends aren't on the road."
– On why San Jose's away record was so much better than its home record through the first few months of the 2007-08 season.

2. "This is our canvas. Our easel. This is how we paint, on fresh sheets of ice."
– On the artistry that is hockey.

1. "It's not my fault (Snow) didn't have any other options coming out of high school. If going to college gets you a career backup goaltender job and my route gets you a thousand points and a thousand games, and compare the two contracts, it doesn't take a rocket scientist to figure out whose decision was better."
– On Islanders goalie Garth Snow's response to Roenick complaining about the officiating during a Flyers-Islanders game during which Snow said Roenick wasn't "that bright." THN

Jeremy Roenick

NHLERS WHO
WENT TO WAR

In honor of men and women, past and present, who have given or are risking their lives for the rest of us, here are the 10 best players who took a leave of absence for military service. Any names not on the list are, of course, not forgotten, nor are their accomplishments both in serving their country and on the ice. – JG

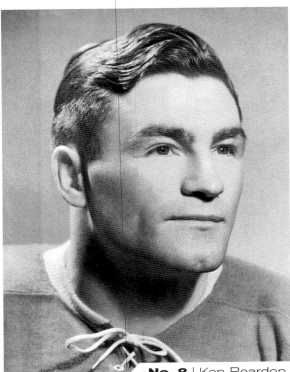

No. 8 | Ken Reardon

10. Woody Dumart

Inducted into the Hockey Hall of Fame in 1992, Dumart was a member of the famed 'Kraut Line' in Boston, all three of whom enlisted in the Canadian Armed Forces during the prime of their careers and didn't return to the NHL for three-and-a-half years. Dumart was a three-time all-star whose NHL career spanned 18 years.

9. Gord Drillon

He played just seven NHL seasons before joining the Canadian military for three years in 1943, but Drillon was one of the most electrifying players of his era. The three-time all-star won the Art Ross and Lady Byng Trophies in 1938 and was inducted into the Hall of Fame in

8. Ken Reardon

Inducted to the Hall in 1966, Reardon was one of the most fearsome and intimidating defensemen of his era. He enlisted in the Canadian Armed Forces after the 1941-42 season and didn't return to the NHL until 1945-46. For his dedication overseas, he was awarded Field Marshall Montgomery's Certificate of Merit for acts of bravery during battle. Reardon was a five-time all-star in just seven NHL seasons.

No. 1 | Milt Schmidt

7. Sid Abel

The center on Detroit's famed 'Production Line' with Gordie Howe and Ted Lindsay, Abel was inducted to the Hall of Fame in 1969. He played parts of 14 NHL seasons, missing two during World War II while with the Royal Canadian Air Force. He was a four-time all-star and won the Hart Trophy in 1949.

6. Turk Broda

Broda was inducted into the Hall of Fame in 1967 after 302 NHL victories with Toronto and two years with the Canadian Armed Forces during the Second World War. He was a three-time all-star and a two-time Vezina Trophy winner.

5. Hobey Baker

The United States' first hockey superstar, Baker played in the old seven-man system as a rover. He was one of the most skilled players of his time and ran roughshod over the collegiate ranks. After starring for Princeton University, Baker played amateur hockey before joining the U.S. Air Force in the First World War and was awarded the Croix de Guerre for his abilities. Baker was killed in a post-war flying accident. The Hobey Baker Memorial Award is given each year to the NCAA's top player.

4. Max Bentley

Bentley was one of three NHL Bentley brothers. He was also one of the best players of his day. He spent two of his prime playing years in the Canadian military during WWII, but still managed to be named an all-star twice, win two scoring titles, a Hart Trophy and a Lady Byng Trophy. He was inducted into the Hall of Fame in 1966.

3. Frank Brimsek

'Mr. Zero' spent 10 seasons in the NHL, nine tending goal for Boston and one with Chicago. Eight of those seasons he was named either a first- or second-team all-star; he also won the Calder Trophy and twice won the Vezina Trophy. He won 252 games and was inducted into the Hall of Fame in 1966. During the Second World War, Brimsek served two years with the U.S. Coast Guard in the South Pacific.

2. Syl Apps

A five-time all-star, Apps won the Calder Trophy and the Lady Byng Trophy during his career, averaging better than a point per game at a time when few managed the feat. The center spent his entire NHL career with Toronto, interrupted by two years in the Canadian Armed Forces during WWII.

1. Milt Schmidt

The most famous NHL war veteran, Schmidt enlisted in the Royal Canadian Air Force in 1942. He lost three-and-a-half years in the prime of his career, was a four-time all-star, and won the Art Ross Trophy and the Hart Trophy an amazing 11 seasons apart. He was inducted into the Hall of Fame in 1961. THN

LOWEST GOAL-SCORING
100-POINT SCORERS

We've got our annual Cy Young watch for guys with far more goals than assists, but were are stumped over what honor to bestow upon the reverse stat line. Best we could come up with is the John Coleman Award (he went 12-48 in 1883 for baseball's Philadelphia Quakers), but that doesn't really do it justice.

Regardless, here are THN's Top 10 lowest-goal-scoring 100-point players. – **JG**

No. 10 | Bobby Clarke

10. Bobby Clarke, Philadelphia, 27 goals, 1974-75

Clarke's Philadelphia Flyers won their second of consecutive Stanley Cups in 1975 and the captain took home the Hart Trophy as NHL MVP. His 89 assists tied Bobby Orr for most in the league, but his 27 goals dropped him to sixth in overall scoring.

9. Ron Francis, Pittsburgh, 27 goals, 1995-96

Francis also scored 27 times, but finished with 92 assists for 119 points, thus he takes ninth here. Francis was the third point of a 1995-96 Penguins triangle that included Mario Lemieux and Jaromir Jagr, Nos. 4, 1 and 2 in league scoring. Along with Lemieux, Francis led the NHL in helpers. (Doug Gilmour also potted just 27 with 84 assists in 1993-94 with Toronto.)

8. Doug Weight, Edmonton, 25 goals, 1995-96

The Edmonton Oilers center turned the trick the same year as Francis, finishing with 25 goals and 104 points, good for 11th in NHL scoring. The 79 assists were a career high and the 25 tallies were one off his top total of 26 in 1997-98.

7. Adam Oates, St. Louis, 25 goals, 1990-91

Remember the old 'Hull and Oates' combination? It couldn't have been on much better display than in '90-91 when Brett Hull had 86 goals (35 more than any other player) thanks in large part to center, Oates, and his 90 assists. Along with 25 goals he finished with 115 points, good for third in scoring.

6. Ron Francis, Pittsburgh, 24 goals, 1992-93

'Ronnie Franchise' set his standard (although with Pittsburgh, not Hartford) during the 84-game '92-93 season when he managed 24 goals and 100 points in the same season that...

5. Craig Janney, St. Louis, 24 goals, 1992-93

...Janney netted 24 goals and 106 points. He was the new Oates in St. Louis, playing setup man to Hull, who had 54 goals that season. It was the only 100-point season of Janney's career.

4. Wayne Gretzky, St. Louis, 23 goals, 1995-96

Because he has more career assists than anyone else has points, people tend to forget 'The Great One' was quite a sniper in his day, hence his lone appearance here. The season he was traded to St. Louis from the Kings (1995-96) was the last 100-point campaign of his career. He finished with 23 goals and 102 points.

3. Adam Oates, St. Louis, 23 goals, 1989-90

Oates gets the nod over Gretzky because he managed his 23-79-102 totals in an 80-game season, rather than an 82-gamer. The 1989-90 season was Oates' first in St. Louis alongside Hull and was also his first 100-point outing.

2. Brian Leetch, Rangers, 22 goals, 1991-92

The only defenseman to make the list, Leetch won the Norris for his 1991-92 efforts. He finished that campaign with 102 points, good for ninth in league scoring. It was his second of five 20-goal seasons, but he'd never come within 15 points of 100 again. We'd still take him on our squad.

1. Joe Thornton, San Jose, 22 goals, 2006-07

Another 22-goal scorer, 'Jumbo Joe' gets top dog status here for netting more points (114) in 2006-07 than Leetch 15 years earlier. It was Thornton's first full season as a Shark coming off his Hart and Art Ross campaign the year before with Boston and San Jose. His 92 assists tie Francis' 1995-96 total for most on our list. THN

No. 1 | Joe Thornton

RIGHT WINGERS

From Flashes to Boom Booms and Flowers to Rockets, THN's Top 10 Greatest Right Wingers of All-time spans across more than 80 years of hockey history.

Some of the most prolific goal-scorers of the past and present make a home here, none any less influential to the development of the game than the next one down the list.

With current Hall-of-Famers and future first-ballot Hall-of-Famers, this list contains elite talent from every decade since the 1920s. *– BD & THN*

10. Teemu Selanne, 1992-active – Winnipeg, San Jose, Colorado, Anaheim

Good things come to those who wait. So while nine teams passed on Teemu Selanne at the 1988 draft, the Winnipeg Jets were willing to reap the rewards once the Finn completed a stint of military service.

In 1992-93, the perseverance paid off. Selanne, a.k.a. 'The Finnish Flash,' became an instant NHL sensation, shattering the record for goals by a rookie by posting an insane total of 76 in 84 games. It was a surprise around the NHL, even to Selanne himself. "My expectations were not that high," he recalled. "I came from Europe, I came from Finland – there were a lot of question marks when I came over."

Though there had been rumblings. Some GMs thought Selanne was the best player available in the 1988 draft, they just didn't want to wait what turned out to be four years for the speedster with great hands. "I was so hungry, too," Selanne said of his breakout campaign. "I wanted to show everyone what I could do."

He scored 40-plus goals seven times, including back-to-back seasons of 50-plus during his first stint with Anaheim. In his second tour with the Ducks, he won his only Cup (2007).

9. Jari Kurri, 1980-1998 – Edmonton, Los Angeles, Rangers, Anaheim, Colorado

Nobody scored more playoff goals during the Edmonton Oilers dynasty years than Jari Kurri, Finland's 'Mr. Hockey.'

Kurri netted 64 goals in 87 post-season games between 1984 and 1988, as the Oilers won four Cups in a five-season stretch. His center, Wayne Gretzky, was second with 55. Kurri's 19 tallies in 1985 are tied with Reggie Leach for the most ever in a single playoff derby. Extend the sample to the seven seasons over which Edmonton claimed five Cups and you'll find Kurri even further ahead of his closest teammate, scoring 77 goals in 116 games to best Glenn Anderson's 58.

Kurri, the first European-trained player to gain 1,000 points in the NHL, remains a revered figure in his home country, where, at 50, he is GM of the national team. "Jari was my idol," Selanne said. "He opened so many doors. People respected Finnish players so much more because of him."

No. 8 | Bernie Geoffrion

Known primarily as Gretzky's trigger man on the right side, Kurri was much more than a one-trick, one-timing pony. He played a cerebral game and could be trusted in all situations. "His all-around game was so good," Selanne said. "He was scoring goals, he saw the game well and his smartness was unbelievable. He and Gretzky, their decision-making was so good."

Kurri's No. 17 has been retired by Team Finland and both the Oilers and his Finnish club, Jokerit, have also taken his sweater out of circulation.

8. Bernie Geoffrion, 1950-1968 – Montreal, Rangers

The Montreal Canadiens are no strangers to elegant pageantry and emotional ceremonies. But for all the spine-tingling banner raisings in their history, few moments could match the raw emotion produced when Bernie 'Boom Boom' Geoffrion's No. 5 was hoisted to the rafters.

The event occurred when the Canadiens hosted the Rangers March 11, 2006. It was the kind of moment Geoffrion – a gregarious, heart-on-his-sleeve type – would have adored. But earlier that morning, just hours before the red carpet was to be unfurled in his honor, Geoffrion lost his brief battle with stomach cancer at age 75.

A tear-soaked ceremony proceeded as planned with Geoffrion's family absorbing the adoration Habs fans showed for a man who's personal and professional life was so tied to the franchise. Helping hoist the banner up that night was Geoffrion's wife of 54 years, Marlene, the daughter of legendary Hab Howie Morenz. Also in attendance were Geoffrion's son, Danny, who played for his dad when the senior coached Montreal briefly in 1979, and Geoffrion's grandson, Blake, a Hobey Baker Award-winner and now a Canadien himself.

The second man in league history to score 50 goals in a season, Geoffrion had more to his game than just the 'Boom Boom' slapper. "He was a good skater, had a good hockey head, played the game (right)," said Hall of Famer Red Kelly. "He was one you couldn't give any opening to or he was going to take advantage of it."

7. Charlie Conacher, 1929-1941 – Toronto, New York Americans

Charlie Conacher had nine brothers and sisters, including Hall of Famers Lionel and Roy. But Charlie was the best and the beast of the Conacher clan – a muscle-bound right winger who had the hardest shot of his era and bowled over opponents with his skill as easily as he did with his brawn.

Conacher broke into the NHL at 19 with Toronto in 1929-30. A member of Toronto's famous 'Kid Line' with Joe Primeau and Harvey 'Busher' Jackson, Conacher used his size (6-foot-1, at a time when the average player height was 5-foot-8) and competitive streak to dominate like few before him had.

Between 1930 and 1936, Conacher led or tied for the league lead in goal scoring five times. He won a Stanley Cup with Toronto in 1932 – that season he scored 34 goals to tie for the lead league, while linemates Jackson led in points and Primeau in assists. "He revolutionized the position because he was so big and so strong," said Kevin Shea, hockey historian and author. "He had a wicked shot...and he was larger than life, even in his retirement years. He socialized with people like Bing Crosby and Bob Hope."

Conacher's ferocious on-ice style took its toll on his body. After nine seasons in Toronto, he was traded to the Detroit Red Wings then the New York Americans, playing three more years. "He went at it 100 percent at all times," Shea said of Conacher, who was inducted into the Hall of Fame in 1961 and died in 1967. "He lived as hard off the ice as he played on it."

6. Brett Hull, 1986-2005 – Calgary, St. Louis, Dallas, Detroit, Phoenix

Who knew the knock on Brett Hull was actually the secret to his success? Fiercely talented and blessed with one of the best shots hockey has ever known, Hull wasn't above whispers that, at times, he wasn't giving his all on the ice.

According to his dad, that's just how Hull played the game. "Brett Hull got more done with less work than anyone I ever saw," said Bobby Hull of his boy.

That's not a father taking a swipe at his son. It's a proud dad declaring his kid operated on an efficient level he himself could never quite reach. "He was the smartest player on the ice, he and Gretzky and Lemieux," Bobby said. "I skated all over the ice to get done what he got done in just a few short strides."

It took more than intelligence for Brett Hull to accomplish what he did. Nobody leads the league in goals for three consecutive years during the offensive heyday of hockey with just smarts on his side. And he was also about more than one-timer bombs. "I happened to have all

86 of his goals (from 1990-91) on tape and it's just amazing, when you watch all of those 86 goals how he scored in so many different ways," Bobby said. "It wasn't all shooting it directly, it wasn't all with his tremendous wrist shot, just getting it and shooting it.

"He was the greatest natural goal-scorer I've witnessed on the ice and I don't care who you talk about."

5. Mike Bossy, 1977-1987 – Islanders

It's hard to believe one of the greatest goal-scorers in NHL history was passed over by 12 teams (Toronto and the Rangers did it twice) before being drafted. But that's exactly what happened to Mike Bossy in 1977.

He potted 309 goals (a Canadian major junior record) in four seasons for the Laval National of the Quebec League, but scouts thought him too timid for the NHL. The New York Islanders couldn't have been happier. "We never had that guy you could count on to break a 2-2 tie," said Islanders teammate and Hall of Famer Denis Potvin. "Mike was that guy."

Bossy became the first NHL rookie to score 50 goals when he netted 53 for New York as a 20-year-old in 1977-78, a record that stood for 15 seasons and is still second all-time. It was the first of his record nine consecutive 50-goal seasons. His five straight 60-goal years are matched only by Gretzky.

Injuries limited Bossy to 10 seasons, but no player has scored at a clip like his: he finished with 573 goals in 752 games, a record .762 goals per game.

Bossy's preternatural ability to score came from lightning-quick release and a knack for always being in the right place at the right time. He was the player the Islanders always looked to pass the puck to, according to Potvin, which helped him become an all-star in eight of his 10 seasons in the NHL (five first team, three second team).

4. Jaromir Jagr, 1990-active – Pittsburgh, Washington, Rangers, Philadelphia

When Jaromir Jagr was drafted fifth overall by the Penguins in 1990, there was doubt the young star would be able to play in the NHL for a couple years. Jagr was under contract with his Czech team, Kladno, and would have to serve in the military before being able to join the NHL.

But that summer, with communism crumbling in Eastern Europe, Czechoslovakia dissolved and Jagr was able to join the Penguins. Pittsburgh was about to turn a corner with other young stars, 25-year-old Mario Lemieux and 22-year-old Mark Recchi, being well complemented by past Stanley Cup champions such as Paul Coffey and Bryan Trottier.

The Penguins defeated the Minnesota North Stars to claim the Stanley Cup and Jagr, at 19, became the youngest player in NHL history to score a goal in the final.

With a big frame and sublime puckhandling skills, Jagr was a superstar in the making. Recognizable by his long mullet, Jagr increased his output – and won another Cup – as a sophomore, then took off with 94 points in Year 3. "He's strong and hard to knock off puck," said Pavel Datsyuk. "He can pass, shoot and can stickhandle; he can do everything."

Jagr's domination of the Art Ross Trophy in the latter half of the 1990s entrenched him among the all-time greats. Leading the league in points for five out of seven seasons between 1994-95 and 2000-01, Jagr also won a Hart Trophy and two Lester Pearson Awards.

3. Guy Lafleur, 1971-1991 – Montreal, Rangers, Quebec

To comprehend the accomplishments and accolades accumulated by Montreal legend Guy Lafleur is to have your breath taken away – not quite to the degree you would seeing the legend known as 'The Flower' (or, to his French-Canadian admirers, 'Le Demon Blond') actually play the game, but close.

Lafleur won five Stanley Cups. He won a pair of Hart Trophies. He won three Art Ross Trophies, three Lester Pearson Awards and one Conn Smythe Trophy. Yet none of those honors could encapsulate what it was to see Lafleur streak up and down arenas for 17 seasons. The right winger was the epitome of what could come from a combination of pure talent and singular dedication. "'Flower' was a hard, hard worker," said Mark Napier, Lafleur's teammate in Montreal for more than five seasons. "Sometimes I'd get to the rink an hour and a half before practice and I'd hear pucks banging off the glass – it was Guy. He'd dumped a pail of pucks and was coming down the right side shooting away with the lights off. He had a joy for the game and that was infectious."

Added Maple Leafs legend Darryl Sittler: "He was a competitive guy. When it was time to score a big goal, he was always the one to do it.

"He was one of those guys like (Bobby) Orr and Gretzky – everywhere they go, they're loved by hockey fans," Sittler said. "Nobody has to tell them what Guy means to the game."

2. Maurice Richard, 1942-1960 – Montreal

Toronto Maple Leafs GM Conn Smythe gave root to one of hockey's great injustices, one that seems to have been perpetuated outside Montreal for decades.

From the time Smythe declared Maurice Richard to be, "just a wartime player," after Richard scored 50 goals in 50 games in 1944-45, the notion has persisted Rocket prospered because the best players were in Europe fighting in the Second World War. (Richard tried to enlist twice and was turned down.)

He scored his 50-in-50 during the war, but led the league in goals four more times after and was also more productive. With 87 goals and 138 points in 112 games, Richard averaged 1.23 points-per-game his first three years. With 457 goals and 1,147 points in 866 games after 1944-45, Richard averaged 1.32 points per game. As Habs coach Dick Irvin said, "The war must still be going on because Richard is still scoring."

His younger brother, Henri, won more Stanley Cups and Jean Beliveau was a more galvanizing leader. But Richard is remembered as the greatest Hab because of the passion he possessed and evoked in those who revered him. "He had great numbers, there is no doubt about that," said hockey historian Eric Zweig, "but he was also a guy who brought people out of their seats better than anyone. It's probably more of a case that you had to see him, that you had to be there."

A state funeral was held for Richard in Montreal when he died in 2000.

No. 3 | Guy Lafleur

1. Gordie Howe, 1946-1980 – Detroit, Hartford

In the fall of 2006, to honor the 60th anniversary of Gordie Howe's debut in a Detroit uniform, owner Mike Ilitch designated the west entrance to Joe Louis Arena as the Gordie Howe entrance.

An odd decision, for the last thing Howe ever did was roll out the welcome mat.

Howe retired in 1971 after 25 seasons in Detroit. He played 1,687 games and scored 786 goals, all team records. After a 1973 comeback to skate with sons Mark and Marty for the WHA's Houston Aeros, Howe returned to the NHL following the 1979 NHL-WHA merger, playing 80 games of 1979-80 with the Hartford Whalers, producing 15 goals and 41 points as a 51-year-old.

Howe could play any type of game – up-tempo, physical, skating. He was at home as a scorer, checker or enforcer. "There was only one Gordie Howe," former NHLer Adam Graves said. "That's why they call him 'Mr. Hockey.' "

Among Howe's firsts are oddities such as: first player to play in the NHL at 50 (1979); first member of the Hockey Hall of Fame to play in the NHL after his Hall induction (1979); and first player to skate on the same team as his sons (1973). "He's absolutely the nicest guy in the world off the ice, but once he put that uniform on, look out," Marty Howe said. "I'm just glad I never had to play against him. Practice was bad enough." ▄▄▄

PLAYERS WHO
MAKE YOU HUNGRY

The NHL's history of players includes many interesting names, including those of professions (i.e. Garth Butcher and Jamie Baker). Others have had the mixed blessing of having a foodstuff in their moniker. These are our favorites, with honorable mentions to Taffy Abel, Cody Almond, Bob Berry, Bill Butters, Joey Crabb, Vern Kaiser, Mark Lamb, Andreas Nodl and Terry Yake. **– AP**

No. 3 | 'Bun' Cook

10. Bob Beers

Given how many hockey players have been known to imbibe the odd bottle of brewed ale, Beers may have the ideal hockey "food name." The former Bruins, Lightning, Oilers and Islanders defenseman was dealt twice in his 11-year pro career – meaning, yes, two different NHL GMs made a trade for Beers. Many people inside and outside the hockey world have made the same transaction.

9. Steven Rice

A former star for Canada at the 1991 IIHF World Junior Championship, Rice steamed NHL executives when he never blossomed in hockey's best league after being drafted 20th overall in 1989. Rice's minutes were limited in 329 career NHL games and he amassed 64 goals and 125 points before retiring at age 27.

8. Andre Champagne

After a junior career at Toronto's storied St. Michael's school, Champagne played only two games at the NHL level, both for the Toronto Maple Leafs. He'd go on to spend most of his decade-long playing career in the American League for Rochester. No telling if he became any more or less bubbly when he did.

7. Adam Oates

One of the most creative playmakers to grace the game, Oates amassed massive offensive numbers in 19 NHL seasons and has more points (1,420) than any U.S. collegiate player in history. Honey, nuts to those who say Oates shouldn't be inducted into the Hockey Hall of Fame.

6. Jim Korn

An American defenseman who played 11 years for five NHL teams, Korn was a bruiser (racking up 1,801 penalty minutes in 596 career regular season games). In many ways, it's amazing he never acquired the nickname "Crack," but perhaps his teammates didn't care.

5. Jari Kurri

A legend of both the NHL and his native Finland, Kurri was a key cog in the Edmonton Oilers dynasty who scored at least 50 goals in a season on four different occasions. He also had some spice in his game, as evidenced by the fact he had more than 100 penalty minutes six times.

4. Paul Coffey

The legendary defenseman earned most of his Hall of Fame numbers with Edmonton and Pittsburgh before bouncing around the league at the end of his 21-year NHL career. In his final season, he had a cup of, er, hot java with Boston, playing 18 games in 2000-01 before retiring as the No. 2 defenseman all-time in goals (396), assists (1,135) and points (1,531).

3. 'Bun' Cook

His given name was Frederick, but everyone knew the left winger as 'Bun' when he skated for the Rangers and Bruins from 1926-37. Part of the 'Bread Line' with his brother Bill Cook and Frank Boucher, 'Bun' won two Stanley Cups with the Blueshirts, went on to coach more American League teams to championships (seven) than anyone else in that league's history and was inducted into the HHOF in 1995.

2. Milan Chalupa

Hockey is the last place you'd expect to find a surname such as Chalupa, but for 14 games in 1984-85, it appeared on the back of a Detroit Red Wings jersey on a defenseman who would never play another game in North America after that. The best part? Chalupa is a Czech!

1. Per Djoos

The standard by which all other hockey/food names are measured, both Djoos' surname (pronounced "juice") and given name (pronounced "pear") are foodstuffs. The Swedish defenseman played only 82 NHL games over three seasons in the early 90s, but his name leaves a legacy bigger and more fruitful than anything he did on the ice.

CHICAGO
BLACKHAWKS

With 85 years of history behind them, it takes a lot to be considered one of the greatest Chicago Blackhawks (or Black Hawks).

Sorry, Doug Wilson – you put up the three highest-scoring seasons ever by a Hawks defenseman and a Norris Trophy to boot, but that's not enough. Steve Larmer, you're the fourth-highest scoring Hawk of all-time and you played 884 straight games in a Chicago sweater – but too bad for you. Jeremy Roenick, you posted three consecutive 100-point seasons in the '90s and endeared yourself to all, but that doesn't mean you make the list.

Nine of the 10 players listed are Hockey Hall of Famers – and the other will be soon enough. – JG

10. Max Bentley

Bentley was as prolific as they came during his six seasons with Chicago in the 1940s – a run interrupted by two years in the military. As a Black Hawk, Bentley won two Art Ross Trophies, a Hart Trophy and a Lady Byng. Along with brother Doug, the Bentleys were one of the most dangerous duos the NHL had seen. Hall of Fame: 1996

9. Ed Belfour

Belfour was incredible in his rookie season with Chicago in 1990-91. He led the league in games played (74), wins (43) – both of which are still team records – and goals-against average, was a first team all-star and won the Calder, Vezina and Jennings Trophies. During the next seven seasons Belfour won another Vezina and three more Jennings. HoF: 2011

8. Chris Chelios

Chelios isn't in the Hockey Hall of Fame yet, but he was one of five members inducted into the U.S. Hockey Hall of Fame in 2011 – and should join the ranks in the main Hall in the near future. A lot of Chelios' best work came while playing in the Windy City. While in Chicago, Chelios won two Norris Trophies was captain for four years, helped the Hawks to the 1992 Cup final and was a five-time all-star in his eight full campaigns with the team.

7. Earl Seibert

If you don't know Earl, you don't know jack. Best remembered as the man who accidentally ended Howie Morenz's career, Seibert was one of the best blueliners of his era, tough as nails and as skilled as anyone. From 1936 to 1944, he made nine straight first or second all-star teams (one for every full season he played with Chicago) – only Mr. Hockey, the Rocket, the Golden Jet and Doug Harvey can boast longer streaks with a single team. HoF: 1963

No. 6 | Tony Esposito

6. Tony Esposito

Speaking of good rookie seasons, how about leading the league in wins, being a first-team all-star, winning the Vezina and Calder and setting a modern record with 15 shutouts? That's what 'Tony O' did in 1969-70. He won two more Vezinas and earned four more all-star berths before retiring as a Hawk in 1984. HoF: 1988

5. Denis Savard

Savard didn't score fewer than 75 points in any of his first 10 years with Chicago. He owns the four highest-scoring seasons in team history and is the franchise's No. 3 all-time point producer. Savard was stuck behind some other pretty decent centers during the 1980s (see: Gretzky, Wayne; Lemieux, Mario) so he never received the league-wide accolades he might have, but he was one of the most exciting players of his generation. HoF: 2000

4. Glenn Hall

Hall played 362 of his 502 consecutive games (without a mask) as a Black Hawk. During 10 seasons with Chicago, Hall won two Vezinas, the Cup in 1961 and was an eight-time all-star – five times a first-teamer. In '61 he played every second of every game, led the league in shutouts and stymied Montreal in Round 1 of the playoffs to dash the Habs' hopes of six consecutive Cups. HoF: 1998

3. Pierre Pilote

Pilote played 821 games with Chicago from 1955 to 1968. He won three consecutive Norris Trophies from '63 to '65 and was an all-star every year from 1960 to 1967, nearly matching Seibert's mark. Pilote captained the team for seven seasons from 1961-1968. HoF 1975

2. Stan Mikita

Mikita is basically Mr. Black Hawk and really should be considered more of 1A than a No. 2 here. He's the Hawks' all-time leader in games played, assists and points and won the Cup in '61. Mikita won four Art Ross Trophies, two Harts, two Lady Byngs and the Lester Patrick Trophy. An eight-time all-star he was the heart and soul of Chicago for 21 seasons. HoF: 1983

1. Bobby Hull

'The Golden Jet' was the greatest goal-scorer of his day. If not for his defection to the World Hockey Association, who knows what his career numbers would look like. He's still 16th all-time in goals scored. While with the Hawks, Hull was a three-time Art Ross winner, won back-to-back Harts in 1965 and '66, won the Lady Byng, the Lester Patrick Trophy and was a 12-time all-star. He was a five-time 50-goal scorer and never tallied fewer than 31 as a Hawk after his second year. HoF 1983

No. 1 | Bobby Hull

PLAYOFF
OVERTIME GOALS

There is nothing quite like scoring the game-winning goal in a professional hockey game. But the intensity and impact of the achievement rises exponentially when the goal is scored in overtime – and again when the overtime period takes place in the playoffs.

*Which are the best playoff overtime goals ever scored in NHL history? Here are our picks for the all-time top 10. – **AP***

No. 9 | Dale Hunter

10. Petr Klima, Edmonton, 1990

It was Game 1 of the Stanley Cup final and three overtime periods were needed before Klima took a feed from Jari Kurri and wired a wrist shot through the legs of Boston's Andy Moog to end the longest game in Cup final history.

9. Dale Hunter, Quebec, 1982

It was the best-of-five, first-ever Battle of Quebec and the deciding game went into overtime. But not for long, as Hunter and Nordiques teammate Real Cloutier had a 2-on-1 on Canadiens goalie Rick Wamsley early in the first overtime and Hunter backhanded a shot in to win the passionately contested series.

8. Pavel Bure, Vancouver, 1994

Canucks defenseman Jeff Brown made a beautiful pass from Vancouver's blueline up the middle to a streaking Bure, who broke in alone on Flames keeper Mike Vernon and scored in double OT to send the Canucks on to the second round (and eventually the Stanley Cup final).

7. Theo Fleury, Calgary, 1991

Fleury had a fantastic career, but one of the things he is most remembered for is his sliding, spinning celebration after he took the puck behind the red line and snapped it between the legs of the Oilers' Grant Fuhr, sending the series to a deciding seventh game.

6. Bobby Nystrom, Islanders, 1980

The first of the Islanders' four Stanley Cups was won on a 2-on-1 Nystrom finished with a backhand tip past Flyers goalie Pete Peeters in the first overtime of Game 6. The Isles retired Nystrom's No. 23 jersey in 1995.

5. Steve Yzerman, Detroit, 1996

Arguably the greatest goal Yzerman ever scored started when St. Louis' Wayne Gretzky couldn't handle the puck at the Detroit blueline. Yzerman grabbed it and raced into the Blues end, firing a perfect shot over the right shoulder of Blues goalie Jon Casey in the second OT of Game 7 of their Western Conference semifinal series.

4. Igor Larionov, Detroit, 2002

When Larionov picked up the puck inside the Hurricanes' blueline in the third overtime of Game 3 of Detroit's Stanley Cup final series against Carolina, he could have passed to teammate Mathieu Dandenault, who was closer to Canes goalie Arturs Irbe on a 2-on-1. Instead, he deked past a Carolina defenseman and scored one of the prettiest backhand goals you'll ever see to give the Red Wings a 2-1 series lead.

3. Pat LaFontaine, Islanders, 1987

The famous Easter Epic game was decided in the fourth extra frame on the flukiest of shots – LaFontaine said he never shot a puck the same way again – and gave the Isles a seven-game series win after they had trailed the series 3-1.

2. Brad May, Buffalo, 1993

May wasn't ever a skilled goal-scorer at the NHL level, but in the first overtime of Game 5 of the Sabres' series against Boston, he took a pass from LaFontaine (who was lying on the ice at the time), deked Hall of Fame blueliner Ray Bourque, then scored past sprawled out Moog to win the first round series. May Day! May Day! May Day!

1. Bobby Orr, Boston, 1970

The measuring stick by which all other playoff and overtime goals are measured, Orr's Stanley Cup-winner was as picturesque as it was timely. It doesn't get any better than seeing hockey's greatest defenseman, arms raised and flying through the air parallel to the ice, after he won it all for the Bruins. ▧

No. 1 | Bobby Orr

MARTIN BRODEUR
RECORDS

Martin Brodeur surpassed many NHL standards once believed to be insurmountable, leaving Glenn Hall's consecutive complete games played (502) as the lone modern goaltender record that will never be neared. (Although Tony Esposito's 15 shutouts in 1969-70 also looks safe.)

In honor of arguably the game's best-ever goaltender, here are Brodeur's 10 most impressive NHL records. – JG

10. Career shootout wins, 42
There are many out there who hate the shootout, saying it's akin to settling a baseball game with a home run derby. But Brodeur's shootout victories have meant 42 more points for New Jersey over the past seven seasons.

9. Wins in a season, 48
New Jersey won 49 games in 2006-07 and Brodeur was the goalie of record for all of them save one. This record is skewed towards the post-lockout era because of the shootout, but it's in the books and Brodeur owns it.

8. Consecutive 40-win seasons, 3
The 40-win plateau has been reached only 46 times. Brodeur did it three years in a row coming out of the lockout and would have done it again the next season if not for sustaining a biceps injury that limited him to 31 games.

7. 40-win seasons, 8
Brodeur's eight 40-win seasons account for nearly 20 percent of the NHL's all-time total. The margin between himself and second place in the category is more than double (Terry Sawchuk, Jacques Plante and Miikka Kiprusoff all have three).

6. Shutouts in one playoff season, 7
Brodeur was nearly unbeatable during the 2003 playoffs, allowing just 41 goals in 24 games and finishing with a 1.65 goals-against average and .934 save percentage. The Devils beat Anaheim for the Stanley Cup, but Brodeur's foe at the other end of the rink, Jean-Sebastien Giguere, was awarded the Conn Smythe Trophy as post-season MVP.

5. Consecutive 30-win seasons, 12
Consistency has been the key to Brodeur's greatness. Yes, you need a consistent team in front of you, but successful NHL squads are built from the crease out. He never had less than 30 wins between 1995 and 2008.

4. Games played, 1,191

Brodeur passed Patrick Roy in this category Dec. 18, 2009 while defeating Ottawa. Prior to 2008-09 season and that biceps injury, Brodeur had played 67 or more games in 12-straight seasons.

3. Most minutes played in a season, 4,697

Brodeur holds three of the five top spots in this category. In 2006-07, he passed his own mark from 2003-04 (since bested again). Brodeur played 78 games in '06-07, the same year he set the record of 48 wins.

2. Shutouts, 119

The latest (if not the greatest) of Brodeur's career marks. He has averaged a shutout every 10 games, not the best ratio in history, but pretty darned good. He topped out at 12 in 2006-07, a number bested only three times since the 1920s.

1. Wins, 656

According to *NHL Official Guide & Record Book*, Brodeur passed Roy with his 552nd victory, but purists waited for Brodeur's 552nd regulation or overtime win to officially pass him the torch. The monumental win came on March 17, 2009 against the Chicago Blackhawks. ▨

Martin Brodeur

HOCKEY MOVIES

As a kid who grew up knowing every word of Slap Shot, *it's next to impossible for anything to top that piece of celluloid history. But the recently released* Goon *is the funniest hockey movie since* Slap Shot *and it's recommend watching for all puck fans (of an adult age).* **– AP**

10. Mystery, Alaska

With arguably the most star-studded cast of actors in any hockey movie – including Russell Crowe, Burt Reynolds, Hank Azaria and Colm Meaney – this film chronicles an Alaskan town bracing for an impromptu game against the New York Rangers. Keep your eye out for cameo appearances from Phil Esposito, Little Richard and Mike Myers.

9. Les Boys

The most successful Quebec-made film series in that province's history began with this movie about an amateur hockey team's comedic exploits. It's not the most original sports movie you'll ever see, but it spawned three sequels and a spinoff TV series because of a joyful approach to capturing the spirit of the game.

8. The Rocket

The story of all-time great Maurice 'Rocket' Richard's ascent to the pinnacle of the sport, this film was made with the help of Richard before he died and features past and current NHLers Vincent Lecavalier, Sean Avery, Pascal Dupuis, Ian Laperriere, Mike Ricci and Stephane Quintal as legends of the past. Don't let the English subtitles scare– the movie was a critically acclaimed hit, winning nine of Canada's Genie Awards, including best actor, actress and director.

7. Sudden Death

Listen, any movie starring 1990s action relic Jean-Claude Van Damme is not going to age well. But this particular film has a lot going for it from a hockey fan's perspective – including cameos from Luc Robitaille, Bernie Nicholls, Markus Naslund and Sidney Crosby's agent Pat Brisson – and registers high on the unintentional comedy scale.

6. The Hockey Sweater

A sentimental favorite, this animated children's movie – about a young Montreal Canadiens fan devastated to accidentally receive a Maple Leafs jersey in the mail – has withstood the test of time. It's only 10 minutes long, but is masterfully told and will tug on any hockey fan's heartstrings long after it's over.

5. Bon Cop, Bad Cop
One of the most financially successful Canadian movies, this film isn't directly about hockey, but its thinly veiled references to the NHL (including fictional commissioner Harry Buttman) make this a more-than-worthwhile puck-related movie.

4. Goon
Jay Baruchel's love letter to the game's tough guys deserves high praise. Both of its main stars, Seann William Scott (of *American Pie* and *Dude, Where's My Car?* fame) and Liev Schreiber (*Scream*, *The Hurricane*) deliver strong performances and the plot isn't ham-fisted as so many sports films are. Hilarious, smart and touching.

3. Miracle
The dramatized story of the 1980 U.S. men's Olympic team is as inspirational now as it was when it was released 24 years after the actual event. Kurt Russell has gained most of his fame for movies like *Escape From New York*, but his work as legendary late coach Herb Brooks was outstanding.

2. Les Chiefs
One of the less mainstream movies on this list is also one of the most affecting. A documentary on a team in the ultra-tough, Quebec-based North American League, this film has more legitimate drama and humor in it than most fictional films about the game. It isn't the easiest movie to get your hands on, but it is absolutely worth the effort.

No. 1 | Slap Shot

1. Slap Shot
What can I tell you? Unless you're a hockey fan who literally is physically allergic to obscenities and cartoonish violence, there's no reason you shouldn't have seen this masterpiece already. It features one of Paul Newman's greatest acting jobs, the immortal Hansons and none of that stinkin' root beer. Honestly, if you haven't seen it, call your local movie rental place (if you still have one), tell them to reserve one for you right @*#$-ing now, then hang up the phone. ▣

POINTS-PER-GAME
SEASONS

*Though Sidney Crosby played only 41 games in 2010-11 and 22 in 2011-12, he posted impressive points-per-game averages at 1.61 and 1.68. Is that good enough to place 'The Kid' on the list of the greatest points-per-game seasons of all-time? Below are the Top 10, with a twist: No player can appear more than once. – **JG***

10. Adam Oates, Boston, 1.69 PPG, 1992-93

Believe it or not, Oates' top scoring season didn't come centering Brett Hull – it came with the Bruins. The most prolific NCAA grad ever led Boston across the board with 45 goals, 97 assists and 142 points in 84 games.

9. Pat LaFontaine, Buffalo, 1.76 PPG, 1992-93

A season of big numbers saw LaFontaine lead the scoring race for much of the campaign, until a certain someone further down the list overtook him at the end. As it was, LaFontaine topped Oates to finish second in scoring thanks to 53 goals and 148 points in 84 games.

8. Bobby Orr, Boston, 1.78 PPG, 1970-71

The greatest defenseman of all-time posted the greatest offensive season of all-time for blueliners. Orr's 37 goals and 139 points in 78 games placed him second in scoring, won him his second of three straight Hart Trophies and his fourth of eight consecutive Norris Trophies. For good measure he finished the campaign with a plus-124, which is still a record.

7. Jaromir Jagr, Pittsburgh, 1.82 PPG, 1995-96

Jagr's 62 goals and 149 points in 82 games represent the 17th-highest point total in NHL history and the top season of his career. It wasn't enough to lead the league, or his team, in scoring, but it's still pretty darn good.

6. Mike Bossy, Islanders, 1.84 PPG, 1981-82

No one in the history of the NHL scored goals at a rate equal to that of Bossy (.762 per contest) and in '81-82 he scored 64 and finished with 147 points in 80 games. He didn't win any regular season awards, but was likely happy with the Stanley Cup and Conn Smythe Trophy he earned in the spring.

5. Bernie Nicholls, Los Angeles, 1.90 PPG, 1988-89

Nicholls had been forging a pretty good career for himself with the Kings, but he exploded for 70 goals and 150 points when The Great One arrived in Los Angeles. 'The Pumpernickel King' never approached those numbers again, but he will always have that season.

No. 4 | Steve Yzerman

4. Steve Yzerman, Detroit, 1.94 PPG, 1988-89

Yzerman's 155 points (65 goals, 90 assists) are the 14th most all-time, but represent the highest total posted by someone not named Gretzky or Lemieux. He won the Lester Pearson Award that season, but was a first- or second-team all-star just once in his career (2000). One can only wonder how many more individual accolades he would have chalked up if he had played in a different era.

3. Phil Esposito, Boston, 1.95 PPG, 1970-71

The guy who kept Orr from winning the scoring title in '70-71 was fellow Bruin Esposito, who put up 76-76-152 totals in 78 games to win the Art Ross Trophy. It was the first time anyone had scored 70 or more goals and stood as the record for 11 seasons until Gretzky potted 92.

2. Mario Lemieux, Pittsburgh, 2.67 PPG, 1992-93

Remember how we mentioned LaFontaine lost the scoring race? Guess who beat him? Lemieux finished with 69 goals and 160 points in just 60 games. Why so few? Oh, just because he was forced to miss two months battling Hodgkin's Lymphoma. If not for that, he would have challenged the single-season goals and points marks set by...

1. Wayne Gretzky, Edmonton, 2.77 PPG, 1983-84

The greatest scorer in history set the record for points per game by tallying 87 goals and 118 assists for 205 points in 74 games. None of those marks represent records (92, 163 and 215 set the pace) and 205 points are "only" the fourth-most ever. Gretzky owns nine of the 11 highest single-season point totals. Lemieux slots in at Nos. 5, 8, 12 and 13. ▥

No. 1 | Wayne Gretzky

OLYMPIC RECORDS

The Olympic Games haven't always offered high drama. There were some serious blowouts over the years. The all-time Olympic goal leader, for instance, is Canada's Harry Watson with 36 tallies. Watson scored all of those goals at the 1924 tournament in Chamonix, France, one in which the Canadians outscored their opponents 132-3 in six – yes, six – games. (And you thought the women's results were lopsided.)

We've drawn the dividing line between the early and modern eras at 1956. That's the year the Soviet Union skated onto the international hockey scene and began its reign as the preeminent international hockey power and any record book without the Soviets is hardly worth noting (sorry, Mr. Watson). Also, by '56 a number of countries could boast top international teams.

So we present THN's Top 10 Olympic records of the "modern era." – JG

No. 8 | Vladislav Tretiak

10. Most points, one game

Czechoslovakia's Vaclav Nedomansky posted six goals and eight points against Poland in 1972 at Sapporo, Japan; the six goals are also the standard for goals in a single contest. But the Poles weren't exactly a powerhouse that year – they were 0-5-0 and outscored 39-9 – which is why Nedomansky's record leads off here.

9. Most points, one tournament

Canada's Fred Etcher set this mark with nine goals and 21 points in 1960 at Squaw Valley, Calif.; Etcher's 12 assists are also tied for the most ever in a single tournament. Like Nedomansky, Etcher's opposition wasn't always the toughest – opponents included Japan in group play and West Germany in the final round – but Canada did only win silver, so Etcher beats out Nedomansky.

8. Most goalie games played, career

The Soviet Union's legendary Vladislav Tretiak leads with 19 Olympic appearances during four Games from 1972 to 1984, earning three golds and a silver for his troubles and finishing with a 1.87 goals-against average in 1,000-plus minutes. Tretiak's 17 career Olympic victories are also a record, but we deemed that mark less impressive because NHL and World Hockey Association pros were barred from the Games.

7. Most medals, career

Russian Igor Kravchuk's two gold medals breaks a tie with Czechoslovakia's Jiri Holik; both have four total medals. Kravchuk's first and final medals came 14 years apart. He began with the Soviet Union in 1988 and finished as an NHLer playing for Russia in 2002.

6. Most goals, one tournament

Nikolai Drozdetsky scored 10 goals at the 1984 Sarajevo Games, helping the USSR return to the top of the medal podium. In 1964 at Innsbruck, Austria, Albin Felc of Yugoslavia and Japan's Masahiro Sato both notched 12 goals, but did so in the B Pool, so we give Drozdetsky the edge.

5. Lowest goals-against average, career

Lots of Soviets and Russians in the Top 10 and this category is no exception. Mikhail Shtalenkov played 13 games for Russia during two Olympics – the 1992 Albertville (France) and 1998 Nagano (Japan) Games – finishing with a 1.64 GAA.

4. Most assists, career

Best known on the west side of the Atlantic for having his ankle broken by Bobby Clarke during the 1972 Summit Series, Valeri Kharlamov is to Russia what Maurice Richard is to Canada – an original superstar. Kharlamov totalled 22 assists in three Olympics from 1972 to 1980, cementing himself as the greatest Olympic set-up man ever.

3. Most Olympic tournaments

Few things are more impressive than longevity, something Finland's Raimo Helminen had in spades. Helminen played in an amazing six Olympic tournaments, beginning in Sarajevo in 1984 as a 20-year-old and ending in Salt Lake City, Utah in 2002 as a 38-year-old. Not surprisingly, Helminen's 39 Olympic games is also a record.

2. Most goals, career

Sweden's Sven 'Tumba' Johansson was voted Sweden's greatest player ever in 1999 for good reason. Although he did play at the 1952 Oslo (Norway) Games, we're going to say his 25 Olympic goals are good because he's classified as a "modern-day" player (he also played at Innsbruck in '64). 'Tumba' led the Tre Kroner to bronze and silver medals during his career.

1. Most points, career

This record was set at the 2010 Olympics to a decidedly little amount of fan fare. But with his second assist of the Vancouver Games, Teemu Selanne passed Kharlamov and Czechoslovakia's Vladimir Bastalik (who also played in the Oslo Games). The 'Finnish Flash' has 37 points (20 goals, 17 assists) in 31 games. THN

No. 1 | Teemu Selanne

BOSTON BRUINS

The Boston Bruins have won only six Stanley Cups in their 88-year history, which is pretty remarkable considering some of the mind-boggling individual talent they've had over the years. In fact, if you were picking a Bruins all-time team, a top-four defense corps of Bobby Orr with Eddie Shore and Ray Bourque paired with Zdeno Chara would be better than any other franchise could produce.

Yes, even better than Doug Harvey, Larry Robinson, Serge Savard and Guy Lapointe. At least that's what we think. Feel free to discuss among yourselves.

*Of course, like their other Original Six partners, the Bruins have a long history to draw on when it comes to putting together lists like this one. But until the Bruins won their first Cup in 39 years in 2011, there hadn't been much recent history to augment the list. But Chara has certainly done enough with the Bruins to be included in this group of magnificent players. – **KC***

10. Dit Clapper
Clapper was the first 20-year player in NHL history and might be one of the most underappreciated. After establishing himself as one of the league's top offensive producers, Clapper moved to defense from right wing and played the blueline the last nine years of his career. At 6-foot-2 and 200 pounds, Clapper was considered a behemoth during his era. Hall of Fame: 1947

9. Zdeno Chara
With six 40-point seasons and a Norris Trophy to his credit with the Bruins, Chara has established himself as one of the best two-way defensemen of his generation. His ability to log huge minutes and anchor the blueline have made him a constant contender for the Norris. Chara cemented his legacy with the Bruins by leading them to the Stanley Cup in 2011.

8. Frank Brimsek
No player in NHL history has ever done, or likely will ever do, what Brimsek did in his first campaign. The man known as 'Mr. Zero' recorded 10 shutouts in his rookie season and became the first and only player in history to win both the Calder and Vezina Trophies and lead his team to the Stanley Cup. When Brimsek was at the height of his career, at the age of 28, he left the Bruins to join the war effort for two years, serving with the U.S. Coast Guard on a patrol boat in the south Pacific. HoF: 1966

7. Johnny Bucyk
Even though Bucyk won two Lady Byng Trophies, he personified a power forward before the term ever existed. Most of his best work came near or in the crease, the place from where he scored the vast majority of his 545 goals with the Bruins. Bucyk didn't win his first Stanley Cup with the Bruins until he was 35 and didn't post his first 50-goal season until he was 36. HoF: 1981

No. 7 | Johnny Bucyk

6. Bill Cowley

When Cowley retired in 1947, he did so holding the record for assists in a season and as the NHL's all-time leading scorer. Yet you rarely hear his name mentioned when it comes to the pantheon of great Bruin players. We're out to change that. This guy was not quite the Wayne Gretzky of his generation, but he was an outstanding talent who helped the Bruins to two Stanley Cups. HoF: 1968

5. Milt Schmidt

If there had been a Selke Trophy in the 1940s, you can bet Schmidt would have had his name engraved on it several times. One of the greatest captains in the history of the franchise, Schmidt gave no quarter when it came to physical play despite his small stature, but he used his hands to win one scoring championship and help the Bruins to two Stanley Cups. HoF: 1961

4. Phil Esposito

Because he was never blessed with much speed or skating skills, Esposito had no choice but to slow the game down. Although he was credited with an inordinate number of garbage goals during his career, there was simply not a more dangerous player around the net than Esposito and his ability to score from in tight with seemingly no room was uncanny. He was also one of the greatest leaders in the history of the game. HoF: 1984

No. 1 | Bobby Orr

3. Raymond Bourque

The only player on the top 10 list to never win a Stanley Cup with the Bruins, Bourque spent most of his career trying to live up to the legacy left by Bobby Orr and Eddie Shore. And he did a pretty darn good job of it. For much of his career in Boston, Bourque was as smooth as silk and versatile. His 17 consecutive seasons as either a first- or second-team all-star selections is a record that not even Gordie Howe or Wayne Gretzky was able to match. HoF: 2004

2. Eddie Shore

Perhaps the only thing keeping Eddie Shore from being considered as good as Bobby Orr was the absence of the Norris Trophy when he played and the lack of all-star teams until his fifth season in the NHL. After all, Shore won four Hart Trophies as the league's MVP, something Orr never accomplished. Shore was simply the best offensive and defensive defenseman of his era and combined skill and brutality like no other blueliner in history. HoF: 1947

1. Bobby Orr

The consensus choice as the greatest defenseman in NHL history – and in some quarters the greatest player in NHL history – is the natural choice as the best Bruin of all-time. No player controlled the pace of the game the way he did, nor was the gap between the best player in the NHL and the rest ever bigger than it was between Orr and all the others when he played. The fact he accomplished so much in only nine full seasons of NHL hockey makes it all the more special. HoF: 1979

SINGLE-SEASON
GOAL-SCORERS

When the puck sneaks past the netminder and a goal is scored, the air in the arena gets thick with excitement and anticipation. You can feel the goalie's despair and the scorer's sense of victory. Players who deliver that excitement on a regular basis are a rare breed and are never forgotten.

To make it to the top of the goal-scoring greats requires an immense amount of hard work, talent and consistency. It's a tough nut to crack, so tough in fact, the last time anyone joined the list was in at the end of the 1992-1993 season when Teemu Selanne logged 76 goals in Winnipeg.

But to be fair to players not named Wayne and Brett, we decided individuals could only appear on this list once. So we went with career-best totals. – JG

No. 10 | Lanny McDonald

10. Lanny McDonald, Calgary, 66 goals, 1982-83

Bet you didn't think 'The Moustachioed One' would be on the list. McDonald was a spry 30 – still young by today's standards, but nearing the end a quarter-century ago – when he notched 66, the 22nd-most in NHL history. Only Wayne Gretzky potted more that season.

9. Mike Bossy, Islanders, 69 goals, 1978-79

No player has a higher career goals-per-game average than Bossy's .762. He was a 21-year-old sophomore when he hit his career high, 10 more than the No. 2 sniper that season, Marcel Dionne. Bossy hit 60-plus goals four more times during his too-short career and only dropped below 50 once, during his 10th and final season, when he managed 38 playing with a back wracked by pain.

No. 7 | Jari Kurri

8. Bernie Nicholls, Los Angeles, 70 goals, 1988-89

Nicholls had put up some big numbers prior to '88-89, averaging 38 goals the previous five seasons. But with the arrival of The Great One in La-La-Land, Nicholls went all 'Pumper-Nicholl,' posting a total only Mario Lemieux could better that year.

7. Jari Kurri, Edmonton, 71 goals, 1984-85

Kurri's best season saw him pot 71 goals and 135 points, but that still wasn't good enough to lead the league (or his team) in either category. His center – you can likely guess who – netted 73 goals and 208 points. Kurri's goal total is good for fourth-most by a right winger and the 10th-most all-time.

6. Teemu Selanne, Winnipeg, 76 goals, 1992-93

Amazingly enough the 'Finnish Flash' reached 76 goals as a rookie, smashing Bossy's 15-year-old freshman record by 23. Selanne has never come close to 76 again, but is a seven-time 40-plus goal-scorer with 663 total tallies.

5. Phil Esposito, Boston, 76 goals, 1970-71

Espo's 76 began a streak of five seasons during which he averaged 65 goals a year, cementing his place as the greatest goal-scorer the NHL had known to that point. Johnny Bucyk scored the second-most goals that season, 51 and measly in comparison. If the Rocket Richard Trophy had existed in the 1970s, Esposito would have won it by an average of 14 goals each of those five seasons.

4. Alexander Mogilny, Buffalo, 76 goals, 1992-93

Mogilny's 76 ranks higher on the list thanks to the amount, 77, of games he played – Selanne played 84 games, Esposito 78. Mogilny was just 24 when he reached 76 and it seemed the sky was the limit. He wouldn't come within 22 goals of his career high again, but still wowed fans with his sublime skill for years.

3. Mario Lemieux, Pittsburgh, 85 goals, 1988-89

No. 3 on this list, No. 4 all-time, the Magnificent One's best goal total came during his best all-around statistical season – he scored 199 total points, fifth-most ever. Lemieux scored 40-plus goals five more times (including 69 twice), but only played 70 or more games twice more during his career. Arguably the most talented player in history, one can only imagine the point totals he would have reached if not for a career interrupted by injury, a three-year sabbatical and cancer.

2. Brett Hull, St. Louis, 86 goals, 1990-91

For a guy drafted 117th overall, the 'Golden Brett' did all right for himself. Hull scored at least 25 goals 16 times during his career, topped 40 goals eight times, 50 goals five times and managed 70-plus three times. His 741 grand total NHL goals rank third all-time behind only Gordie Howe and Gretzky and his 86 in '90-91 is third-most behind – you guessed it – two of Gretzky's seasons.

1. Wayne Gretzky, Edmonton, 92 goals, 1981-82

It's fitting that the highest-scoring player (in terms of goals, assists and points) in history sits No. 1 on this list. Gretzky owns four of the 10 highest single-season goal scoring marks. No player has more consecutive seasons of scoring 40 goals (12) or 60 goals (four, all 70-plus) and no player has scored three-or-more goals in a game (50) or in a season (10) more than The Great One. He also scored 20 goals 17 times, 13 in a row; 30 goals 14 times; 50 goals nine times, eight in a row; and 60 goals five times. THN

GORDIE HOWE
ACHIEVEMENTS

When dissecting the dynamic career of Gordie Howe, where do you start?

He played 26 years as an NHLer, skating in the league as a teenager and into his 50s. His most productive season in the NHL came after he turned 40. He won the Hart Trophy at the age of 35.

As former NHLer Adam Graves once put it, "There's only one Mr. Hockey."

In recognition of Howe's one-of-a-kind career, let's look back at his 10 greatest achievements. – BD

No. 9 | Marty, Gordie & Mark Howe

10. Statement game

During a Feb. 1, 1959 game at Madison Square Garden, Howe destroyed the face and reputation of New York Rangers defenseman Lou Fontinato, at the time considered the NHL's toughest customer. When their fight was done, Fontinato's nose was broken and listing badly to one side.

9. Family affair

On June 19, 1973, two years into retirement after a quarter-century as a Detroit Red Wings right winger, Howe, 45, announced he would end his retirement to come back and play with his sons Mark and Marty for the WHA's Houston Aeros. In his first season, Howe recorded 100 points, was named MVP of the league and the Aeros won the Avco Cup title.

8. Fifty(-two) and fabulous

After the 1979 NHL-WHA merger, Howe, 52, played one more NHL season for the Hartford Whalers, scoring 15 goals during the 1979-80 campaign. Only 171 NHL players managed to reach the 15-goal plateau in 2011-12. None were eligible for AARP benefits.

7. Welcome home

Howe played in a record 23 NHL All-Star Games, but none were more significant than the last one, on Feb. 5, 1980. Skating in the mid-season classic at Joe Louis Arena as a Whaler, a capacity crowd of Red Wings fans brought Howe to tears with a four-minute standing ovation during pre-game introductions.

6. Goal oriented

Playing the majority of his career in a six-team league where checking was tight and scoring was rare, Howe still collected 801 career NHL goals, which remains the league mark for a right-winger. He led the NHL in goal scoring five times.

5. Straight shooter

Jumping his career-high output in goals from 16 to 35, Howe finished third in NHL scoring during the 1949-50 season, posting the first of his NHL-record 22 straight 20-goal seasons. In five of those seasons, he collected at least 40 goals, counting a minimum of 30 times on another nine occasions.

4. First to four digits

Setting up a goal by Howie Glover Nov. 27, 1960 in a 2-0 shutout of the Toronto Maple Leafs, Howe became the first player in NHL history to record 1,000 career points. Eight years would pass before Montreal's Jean Beliveau would become the second.

3. Playoff payoff

Leading Detroit to the Stanley Cup in the spring of 1955, Howe recorded nine goals and 20 assists in 11 games to wipe out the single-season playoff scoring mark of 19 points established in 1919 by Montreal's Newsy Lalonde. Over the next 15 years, only Chicago's Stan Mikita (21 in 1961-62) would top Howe's total.

2. Golden oldie

At the age of 41, when most players were already enjoying retirement, Howe enjoyed a career year. Skating on a line with Alex Delvecchio and Frank Mahovlich, Howe posted a career-best 103 points, including 44 goals, which tied for the third-highest output of his career.

1. Top class

Finishing third in the Art Ross Trophy race behind 'Production Line' teammates Ted Lindsay and Sid Abel, Howe launched an NHL mark that will never be equalled: 20 years among the top five league scorers. Howe's streak ended in 1969-70, when his 71 points were only good enough for ninth overall. Consider that Wayne Gretzky owns second on this list with 13 top-five finishes in succession and you understand how insurmountable this standard will prove to be. THN

No. 1 | Gordie Howe

BIZARRE NHLER
BIRTHPLACES

By and large, elite hockey players have come from Canada, the United States, Russia and a handful of European countries. However, more than a few NHL players came into the world in the most unlikely of locations. **– AP**

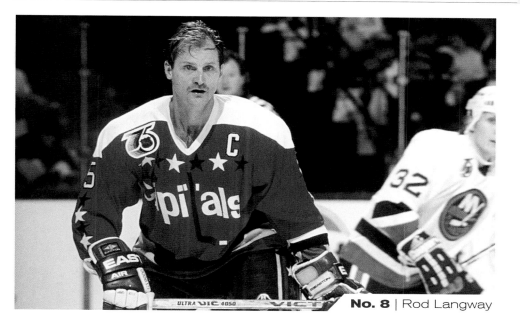

No. 8 | Rod Langway

10. Olaf Kolzig, Johannesburg, South Africa

The long-time Capitals goalie was born to German parents in South Africa's largest city, but spent his formative years in Canada. Johannesburg claims to be the lightning capital of the world – and the Lightning was the final team Kolzig played a game for.

9. Ed Beers, Zwaag, Netherlands

Beers was a standout scorer for the Flames in the early 1980s and was born in this town in North Holland founded in the 13th century.

8. Rod Langway, Taipei, Taiwan

The sole Hockey Hall of Famer on this list, Langway remains the only NHLer ever born in the Republic of China. His father was a U.S. serviceman stationed in Taiwan at the time of his birth, but he grew up in Massachusetts.

7. Paul MacLean, Grostenquin, France

Like Langway, MacLean's father was a military man, but instead for Canada. MacLean, currently the coach of the Ottawa Senators, was born at an air force base before moving at age two to his eventual home in Antigonish, N.S.

6. Robyn Regehr, Recife, Brazil; Richie Regehr, Bandung, Indonesia

The Regehr Bros. were born to Mennonite missionary parents. Robyn lived in Brazil for his first three years before relocating to Indonesia, where Richie was born. The family moved back to Canada four years later.

5. Rumun Ndur, Zaria, Nigeria

The former NHL enforcer last played in hockey's top league for Atlanta in 1999-2000, but also skated in various North American minor pro leagues and U.K. league games. He was born in Africa, but grew up in Ontario.

4. Chris Nielsen, Moshi, Tanzania

Nielsen, who played 52 NHL games for Columbus from 2000-02, was born to Canadian diplomat parents in the East African nation. Moshi is located near the bottom of Mt. Kilimanjaro and now hosts a marathon every February.

3. Rick Chartraw, Caracas, Venezuela

The veteran defenseman of 420 NHL games, mostly with the Canadiens, was born in South America when his dad worked there as an engineer. That he wound up in Montreal was in one sense very appropriate, since Caracas once was known for its red-tiled roofs.

2. Craig Adams, Seria, Brunei

Adams, a Stanley Cup winner with Carolina (2006) and Pittsburgh (2009) was born in this nation on the Island of Borneo in Southeast Asia while his father was on business with Shell Oil. Seria is a key cog in the oil and gas industry in Brunei and was one of the main hot spots in a rebellion against the British Army in late 1962.

1. Ed Hatoum, Beirut, Lebanon

Hatoum was born in Lebanon's capital in 1947 and emigrated with his family to Ottawa 10 years later. He played 47 NHL games for Detroit and Vancouver before spending the majority of his career in the minor leagues. 🅣🅗🅝

No. 2 | Craig Adams

WINNIPEG JETS

Winnipeg once again has an NHL franchise, but let's not forget the team's original incarnation. The Jets now have a new logo, new arena and…a new record book.

When the organization moved to Phoenix back in 1996, they took the history of the club with them, meaning the Coyotes' all-time leading scorer is, strangely, Dale Hawerchuk. The new Jets? Ilya Kovalchuk tops their list.

But let's go back to a simpler, less confusing time and remember who first made Winnipeg great. Here are the top 10 original Jets of all-time. **– AP**

10. Paul MacLean

In seven years as a Jet, MacLean scored fewer than 30 goals in a season just once and that was when he played only 69 games (and scored 27) in 1985-86. He also had three 40-goal campaigns and will be remembered as one of the most offensively skilled Winnipeg wingers ever.

9. Dave Babych

The 19-season veteran D-man began his NHL career in Winnipeg in 1980 and made an immediate impact with 44 points. He followed that up with a career-high 74-point performance in his third pro season. In 390 games as a Jet, Babych amassed 73 goals and 321 points.

8. Keith Tkachuk

One of just four American-born NHLers to score 500 goals, Tkachuk posted 28 goals and 51 points in his rookie year and 41 goals and 81 points in his sophomore season. His 50-goal season in 1995-96 was the team's highest point in its final season in Winnipeg.

7. Phil Housley

After spending his first eight NHL seasons in Buffalo, Housley came to the Jets in a blockbuster trade for Dale Hawerchuk in 1990. Although he played just three seasons in Winnipeg, Housley played in the All-Star Game in all three and averaged 65 assists and 86 points a year with the franchise.

6. Anders Hedberg

The native Swede was a major force for the Jets in the four years he was with the franchise (when it was still a part of the World Hockey Association). Hedberg had at least 50 goals and 100 points in each year, including a career-best 70-goal, 131-point campaign in 1976-77.

5. Ulf Nilsson

Nilsson spent the same four WHA seasons with the Jets as his countryman and linemate Hedberg and did just as much damage to the opposition while he was there. In Nilsson's first year he had 120 points and never had fewer than 114 in any season in Winnipeg.

No. 7 | Phil Housley

4. Thomas Steen

Arguably the most beloved Jet ever, Steen played 950 games with the franchise and never wore a different NHL uniform. He amassed 817 points in 14 seasons, the best of which came in 1988-89 when he scored 27 goals and 88 points.

3. Teemu Selanne

Selanne ended his Jets career with 147 goals and 306 points in only 231 games, but will be most remembered in Winnipeg for his record-smashing 76-goal rookie season. Like Steen, he is utterly adored to this day by Winnipeggers.

2. Bobby Hull

One of the greatest offensive forces in hockey history, Hull scored 307 goals and 648 points for the Jets in 429 games (all but 18 of which took place in the WHA), including a career-high 77 goals and 142 points in 1974-75. Hall of Fame: 1983

1. Dale Hawerchuk

Hawerchuk made an unforgettable first impression – under the pressure of being a No. 1 overall draft pick, no less – scoring 45 goals and 103 points in his rookie campaign of 1981-82 with the Jets. For the next eight seasons, he would shine brighter than any other Winnipeg player, posting five 100-plus point seasons and becoming the franchise's all-time leading scorer with 929 points. HoF: 2001 THN

No. 1 | Dale Hawerchuk

THINGS YOU ALWAYS
HEAR ON DRAFT DAY

The NHL draft has had its fair share of surprises. In the 1974 draft, for instance, Punch Imlach, then the Buffalo Sabres GM, called out a name that nobody had heard before – Taro Tsujimoto of the Tokyo Katanas.

One problem: no such player existed. Imlach was just bored with the process and wanted to have some fun. The selection, however, was made official and will forever go down in history.

Unfortunately, the draft isn't always that interesting. In fact, much of it is formulaic, like these 10 things you will always hear.

It all starts when NHL commissioner Gary Bettman steps up to the podium to address the local crowd. It wouldn't matter if Bettman just finished pulling a bunch of babies out from a burning building, he'd get booed.

Predictably, Bettman will counter with some kind words for the local NHL organization and the great fans of that team. The response will be a smattering of applause. Welcome to the NHL draft. **– BC**

10. "Boooooooooooooooooo."
The draft's a happy day, but don't tell that to the partisan crowd.

9. "With the (insert number) pick in the year's NHL draft, the (insert team) select, from the (insert junior or college team) of the (insert league), (insert player)."
It's basically Mad Libs with prospects.

8. "We think he's a very special player."
Even though it's an individual speaking, "he" uses the word "we" with regularity because it's all about "the team."

7. "We'd like to congratulate the (insert team)'s organization on their Stanley Cup championship."
A sentence always spoken through gnashed teeth.

6. "Hello to our fans at the draft party back in..."
It's important to communicate in a long-distance relationship.

5. "I'm going to work hard in the summer, give 110 percent in training camp and see what happens."
Math never got in the way of a prospect making a team.

4. "We're very proud to select..."
Deadly sins be damned.

3. "We'd like to congratulate (insert names) on their recent induction into the Hockey Hall of Fame."
It's good to mix the old with the new.

2. "We had him ranked higher. We didn't expect to get him where we did in the draft."
There's that "we" again.

1. "We'd like to thank the city of (insert city), the organization and the fine fans of (insert city) for hosting these festivities."
They can't hear you over the booing. ▄▄▄

NHL Draft Day

2011-12 NHLERS AS SELECTED BY NHLERS

It can be easy for critics to watch from the stands and grade their favorite players. It's much more insightful to get rankings courtesy of the players, who ultimately are in the best position to judge others within the game.

In order to create this list, in late 2011 and early in 2012 we polled 150 NHLers, five from each team. (Players could not vote for teammates.) The votes were tabulated using a weighted system.

*And, if you can believe it, one of our top 10 decided to hang 'em up this summer. It's good to go out on top, eh? – **THN Staff***

10. Zdeno Chara, Boston

The son of an Olympic wrestler, Chara is easily the most intimidating defenseman in the world. At 6-foot-9 and 255 pounds, he has Norris Trophy skill and devastating physical tools.

"It's not fun," said Buffalo Sabres captain Jason Pominville of playing against Chara. "There aren't many like him that are that big, with that good of a reach. The only thing tougher than trying to get around him or away from him in the corner is blocking one of his shots. You know they're going to hurt before they even hit you."

And lord help you if you upset the man. Most enforcers won't even challenge the Bruins' behemoth to a fight.

9. Daniel Sedin, Vancouver

Daniel showed a remarkable amount of restraint (perhaps too much, really) during the infamous punch buffet Boston's Brad Marchand subjected him to in the 2011 Stanley Cup final. If only the left winger had the same mercy on goaltenders.

The finisher of the Sedin twins show, Daniel is an Art Ross Trophy and Ted Lindsay Award winner and, like his brother, Henrik, is far from a weakling on the ice. "Over the years they've gotten stronger physically," said Jarome Iginla. "They're strong on their feet and sticks. Definitely one of the top lines in the league."

Daniel has the scoring title to match Henrik's, but trails him by a Hart Trophy in the hardware race.

8. Alex Ovechkin, Washington

You could certainly make the case Ovechkin hasn't improved one iota since taking the league by storm in the 2005-06 season. In fact, you could easily make the case the two-time Hart Trophy winner's game has regressed.

But that he is still on this list indicates the high level at which he was performing before. Let's face it – his mediocre is still pretty darn good.

No. 5 | Jonathan Toews

He is predictable, but that doesn't mean you can always stop coming down his left wing. "He has speed, power and skill and he's a threat to shoot all the time," said Florida Panthers defenseman Brian Campbell said. "You want to stay close to him all the time."

7. Nicklas Lidstrom, Detroit

It wouldn't have been a surprise whatsoever if Lidstrom made this top 10 list again had he come back for another season in 2012-13. No one will ever match his sustained excellence. His superior intellect, skill and deadly accurate shooting and passing were on display for 20 seasons.

He played almost every game, played a ton and did it all at a sublime level. As fellow Swedish D-man Erik Karlsson said in early 2012: "Every game he seems to do the same things over and over again and it seems to be working over and over again."

In addition to his four Stanley Cups, he also owns a gold medal from the 2006 Olympics. Oh, and of course there are those seven Norris Trophies.

6. Evgeni Malkin, Pittsburgh

Malkin can probably do the butterfly in the pool better than any player in NHL. Check it out on YouTube and you'll see what we mean. But on the ice he stings like a bee.

With the extended absences of fellow centers Sidney Crosby and Jordan Staal in 2011-12, Malkin put together an MVP-caliber season and continues to get stronger. He's become tougher along the boards and in the corners.

He almost single-handedly resurrected James Neal's career and willed the Penguins to the upper half of the Eastern Conference. "Right now, he's probably the best player in the league," Flyers blueliner Kimmo Timonen said.

5. Jonathan Toews, Chicago

Putting aside Toews' outstanding accomplishments so far in his career – world juniors gold, Stanley Cup, Conn Smythe Trophy, Olympic gold – it's the words of his peers that indicate arguably the most complete player in the game is still improving.

"He can hurt you in so many ways," said Predators defenseman Kevin Klein of the 23-year-old center. "Offense or defense, it doesn't matter. And it's amazing to see a guy with that much skill be so committed to playing as hard as he does in all parts of the ice. You try your best to contain him, but it's extremely tough."

Despite a 2011-12 campaign shortened by a concussion, Toews still managed 57 points in 59 games, good enough to place him fourth on the Blackhawks scoring chart.

4. Steven Stamkos, Tampa Bay

Not only has Stamkos quickly become one of the faces of the NHL, but he is the poster boy for a new way of thinking.

As the first breakout success story of Gary Roberts' training and nutrition regime, the Bolts center has become a beast on the ice and a scoring machine – only the fifth NHLer ever with three 40-goal seasons before his 23rd birthday – thanks in part to off-season sled pulls and unbalanced weightlifting.

"His shot is pretty impressive and he gets it off quick," said Washington Capitals defenseman Dennis Wideman. "You have to keep your gap with him as close as possible, because he doesn't need a lot of time to get it off."

3. Claude Giroux, Philadelphia

Giroux, a center, wasn't heralded as the next can't-miss superstar when he made the NHL for good in 2008-09. But in 2011-12, he was the league's third-leading scorer (93 points in 77 games) and the undisputed leader of a young, fearless group of Flyers whose best days have yet to be seen.

"He's a tough competitor," said fellow sniper and former teammate Joffrey Lupul of the Toronto Maple Leafs. "He's gotten better every year and now he's one of the better players in the league.

"He's got all the tools to be a superstar for a long time and you can see how important he's become to that team in a really short period of time. He's dangerous, for sure."

2. Pavel Datsyuk, Detroit

When you talk to Datsyuk, chances are he'll have you doubled over with laughter. He'll surprise you that way, the same way a slight, 5-foot-11 guy can be the best two-way player in the NHL.

With a sense of conviction that matches his sublime skill level, Datsyuk has made a career of pouncing on pucks and not giving them up, winning faceoffs and being a demon defensively.

And then there are the goals – the beautiful, highlight-reel, did-you-see-what-he-just-did goals. "He pulls something out every night that you're not expecting," said St. Louis Blues goalie Brian Elliott, "and you didn't expect to see at all."

1. Sidney Crosby, Pittsburgh

He's played in just 63 games the past two seasons and still mustered up 103 points. And despite all the concussion problems and missed time, Crosby has not been forgotten by his peers.

Lots of players have off-the-charts talent, but what defines Crosby are his absolutely maniacal attention to detail and willingness to become dominant in aspects of the game that were weaknesses.

"A few years ago people ripped on him about faceoffs and his shot," said Toronto Maple Leafs' Colby Armstrong, a former teammate. "Then he comes in and scores 50 goals (in 2009-10) and becomes one of the best faceoff guys in the league. He's so determined to be the player he is."

No. 1 | Sidney Crosby

RULE CHANGES

In brainstorming this list, we waxed poetically about $50 fines for match penalties, eight-man teams and standing-still penalty shots 38 feet from the goal a la football (that's soccer for you colonials). Oh how the game has changed.

And while some rules have come and gone over the years, others remain staples of hockey today, defining the game from end to end. Here are our Top 10 rules that changed the game. – JG

10. Red line introduced, 1943

Prior to this there were just two bluelines and a lot of offside calls. The red line reduced those and sped the game up. The NHL considers the introduction of the red line the beginning of the league's modern era.

9. Video replay, 1991

Today it seems every other goal goes to replay, but it wasn't always so. Video took the guessing out of game-changing events and made sure a goal is really a goal. Just don't tell that to Buffalo Sabres fans...

8. Mandatory helmets, 1979

Although many were already wearing helmets, the days of wind-blown manes began to wane when it was deemed all players entering the NHL must don head protection. The last player to go helmetless was Craig MacTavish. He retired in 1997.

7. Blade regulations, 1969

There was a time when NHLers played with their blades like kids who play in the cul-de-sac. Banana blades were all the rage in the '60s thanks to Bobby Hull and his Black Hawks teammates; pucks flew through the air like supersonic knuckleballs and literally scared goalies into wearing masks. But in 1969 blade curves were restricted to one-inch maximums, a year later they were further reduced to a half-inch.

6. Standardized periods, 1927

Although three 20-minute periods had been around since 1910, stop-time and intermissions were introduced in 1927, making each contest considerably longer (especially since squads could dress a max of 12 skaters at the time). Teams were made to change ends after each period and sudden-death overtime was introduced.

5. Icing, 1937

During the '30s NHL leaders were in tough to average a point per game and if teams scored 2.5 goals per contest they led the league. Icing was introduced to do exactly what it does today, keep panicky teams from simply firing the puck down the ice when on the defensive. The rule remains today just as it was all those years ago.

No. 1 | 1929-30 Boston Bruins

4. One goal on minor penalties, 1956

There was a time when a minor penalty meant two minutes of shame no matter how many times the opposition score, but that changed in '56 thanks to the overwhelming power play of the Montreal Canadiens. With names like Beliveau, Richard(s), Geoffrion and Harvey, the Habs ran a clinical attack that at times was just plain unfair.

3. Stand-up goalie eliminated, 1917

Here's one for you: what would goaltending look like today if the butterfly style was outlawed? Well, there are many stories from the NHL's early days of "goalers" pretending to trip or fall just to go to the ice and have the puck hit them. They'd have to put on a good show, however: netminders were penalized for leaving their feet.

2. Offside rules codified, 1930

In the wake of a huge up-tick in scoring, the NHL realized it had to do something to stanch the flow of players into the offensive zone. Offside, although not a new rule, was refined to basically what it is today. Players were not allowed to enter the offensive zone before the puck and play was blown dead when the rule was broken.

1. Forward passing permitted, 1929

To promote offense, the NHL had experimented earlier in the decade by allowing forward passing in the defensive and neutral zones, but not until the 1929-30 season was it allowed anywhere else on the ice. The result? Scoring more than doubled. Boston became the first team in league history to score 100 goals, but all other teams followed suit that season. The Bruins potted 179 goals to lead the league after managing just 89 the season prior, which also led all teams. Cooney Weiland won the scoring title with 43 goals and 73 points in 44 games. The leader in '28-29, Ace Bailey, had just 22 goals and 32 points. Forward passing birthed the modern game. THN

SINGLE-SEASON
PLAYOFF SHOT-BLOCKERS

With the shot-blocking debate raging during the 2011-12 playoffs – how much is too much? – we took a look into the statistical archives to uncover the most prolific shot-blockers.

As much as we'd like to include shot-blocking greats from the previous generations like Guy Carbonneau, Brad Marsh and Craig Ludwig, the NHL only began to track blocked shots after the 2004-05 lockout.

Despite all the hoopla about blocked shots, only one player from the 2011-12 tournament makes this list. Perhaps shot-blocking isn't quite the scourge some believe it is? We'll let you decide. Here are THN's top 10 single-season playoff shot-blockers (not surprisingly, all are blueliners). – **Taylor Rocca**

10. Alexander Edler, Vancouver, 60, 2011

Edler was a key cog as the Canucks made their way to the Stanley Cup final for the first time since 1994. He averaged more than 24 minutes of ice time during the playoffs, scoring two goals and 11 points in 25 games as the Canucks once again fell one win short.

No. 10 | Alexander Edler

9. Brooks Orpik, Pittsburgh, 61, 2008

During Pittsburgh's first of two straight runs to the final, Orpik led the league with 61 blocks in 20 games. He also led the playoffs with 102 hits as the Penguins lost to the Detroit Red Wings in the final.

8. Ryan McDonagh, New York Rangers, 62, 2012

The 23-year-old McDonagh was a rock during the Blueshirts 20-game run, logging nearly 27 minutes of ice time per game and he looks be blossoming into one of the league's best two-way D-men. Hard to believe Montreal allowed him to slip away...in a trade for Scott Gomez no less. Ouch.

7. Jay McKee, Buffalo, 64, 2006

The rugged, reliable defender finished third in blocked shots in the NHL with 64 in 17 games. McKee also led his team in playoff PIM with 30 as Buffalo lost in the third round. His post-season performance played a big role in earning him a four-year, $16-million free agent deal with St. Louis that summer.

6. Chris Pronger, Edmonton, 66, 2006

Pronger was the man in Edmonton during the spring of '06, to the point many felt he should have won the Conn Smythe despite his Oilers falling in a seven-game Stanley Cup heartbreaker to Carolina. Not only did he finish second on the team in blocked shots, Pronger led the team in scoring with 21 points in 24 games. His plus-10 rating and average of nearly 31 minutes in ice time were also tops.

5. Jason Smith, Edmonton, 67, 2006

Oilers captain Jason Smith was widely regarded as a defensive stalwart throughout his 15-year career. In the Oilers' improbable run to the Stanley Cup final in 2006, Smith led the Oilers with 67 blocked shots in 24 games as Edmonton fell one win short of returning the Cup to Canada.

4. Hal Gill, Montreal, 68, 2010

At 6-foot-7 and 241-pounds, perhaps Hal Gill just got hit by more shots than he actually intended to block. Either way, the Canadiens' behemoth helped Montreal advance to the third round of the playoffs. Gill was also a penalty-killing expert for the Habs, finishing with an average of 3:47 in shorthanded ice time through 18 games, good for second on the team.

3. Chris Pronger, Philadelphia, 71, 2010

The only man to appear twice on this list, Pronger was a key component on multiple Stanley Cup-contending teams over the past decade. After a Cup-final appearance with Edmonton in 2006 and a championship in Anaheim in 2007, Pronger joined the Flyers in 2009-10 and led them to a final date with the Blackhawks. His 71 blocked shots and average ice time of more than 29 minutes through 23 games were both league leaders as the Flyers fell in six games.

2. Dennis Seidenberg, Boston, 74, 2011

The native of Germany enjoyed a coming-out party during the 2011 Bruins' run to the Cup. Seidenberg established himself as a bona fide top-pairing defenseman by pacing all Boston blueliners with 11 points and leading the league in blocked shots in 25 games.

1. Anton Volchenkov, Ottawa, 80, 2007

Always known as a bang-and-crash defensive specialist who's always willing to sacrifice his body, Volchenkov was a shot-blocking fiend in 2007 as Ottawa drove to the Cup final. His 80 blocked shots in just 20 games were tops in the league. To put that stat in perspective: the runner-up, teammate Chris Phillips, blocked 24 less (56). THN

No. 1 | Anton Volchenkov

GAME 7s

"*The intensity and dramatic feeling of a Game 7 is irreplaceable,*" *explained then Dallas Stars goalie Marty Turco to THN in 2009. "You know that either way there's going to be a handshake at the end of the game – and being on the right side of that handshake is the only thing you're focused on.*"

Thanks, Marty, we couldn't have said it better. Here are our favorite do-or-die contests from over the years – **JG**

No. 6 | Ray Bourque & Patrick Roy

10. Toronto 3, Detroit 1 – April 18, 1942

In the first Stanley Cup final to reach a seventh game, the Maple Leafs prevailed, storming back from a 3-1 series deficit to win their first championship in 10 years. They had lost six finals in the meantime.

9. Detroit, 3 Montreal 1 – April 14, 1955

The Canadiens' fifth final in five years ended as it had the year before, with a seven-game defeat to the Red Wings. But this time *Les Glorieux* were without their star, Maurice Richard, who had been suspended for the final three games of the regular season and the entire playoffs after he hit a referee during a brawl. The suspension was the impetus for the 'Richard Riot.' But Habs fans were sated each of the next five years, as their team ran-off five Cups in a row.

8. Toronto 4, Detroit 0 – April 25, 1964

Game 7 was set up by Bob Baun's broken-ankle overtime goal in the sixth game for the Maple Leafs. Johnny Bower recorded his second shutout of the post-season and Toronto won its third Cup in a row.

7. Detroit 2, Montreal 1 (OT) – April 16, 1954

The second and last Cup final Game 7 to go to overtime ended on an 'own goal' by legendary Montreal blueliner Doug Harvey. While attempting to glove a dump-in by Red Wing Tony Leswick, Harvey deflected it into the Montreal net.

6. Colorado 3, New Jersey 1 – June 9, 2001

Joe Sakic accepts the Cup from commissioner Gary Bettman and passes it to Ray Bourque – the first time the Hall of Fame defenseman had touched it. Patrick Roy won his record third Conn Smythe Trophy.

5. Tampa Bay 2, Calgary 1 – June 7, 2004

It couldn't get any closer than this series: Game 7 was won by a single goal and just one goal separated the two teams throughout the series. The Lightning's Ruslan Fedotenko scored both Tampa goals.

4. Montreal 3, Chicago 2 – May 18, 1971

The first of Montreal's six Cups in the 1970s. Henri Richard scored the decisive goal and Ken Dryden became a living legend for winning the Conn Smythe Trophy after playing just six regular season games. Dryden won the Calder Trophy the next season. It took 16 years for the next seven-game Cup final.

3. Edmonton 3, Philadelphia 1 – May 31, 1987

The Flyers rallied from a three-games-to-one deficit to take it to Game 7 and the Oilers rallied from 1-0 down to win the game. Despite the loss, Philly's rookie netminder Ron Hextall won the Conn Smythe Trophy.

2. Detroit 4, Rangers 3 (2OT) – April 23, 1950

The longest Game 7 in Cup final history was also the first to go to extra time. Pete Babando scored at 8:31 of the second overtime to clinch Detroit's fourth Cup.

1. Rangers 3, Vancouver 2 – June 14, 1994

The Presidents' Trophy-winning Blueshirts ended a 54-year Cup drought on Mark Messier's fourth game-winning goal and 30th point of the playoffs. Brian Leetch won the Conn Smythe Trophy after leading all players in post-season assists and points. ▨

No. 1 | Mark Messier

ARENAS

They used to call arenas 'barns' back in the day. That sort of made sense, considering in some instances that was how they felt.

The old Maple Leaf Gardens had trough-style urinals fit for the finest horses. Pittsburgh's Mellon Arena featured a dome-like roof and folding chairs in the visiting dressing room. New York's Madison Square Garden actually relocated playoff games once because the circus was in town.

Say what you will about the smell – they had character.

Not that today's shiny new arenas are totally without charm; you just have to dig beneath the private luxury boxes and corporate logos to find it. And, of course, NHL buildings are about more than just bricks and mortar – the fans play a big part in what makes them great. Here are some of the better current ones. – MT

No. 10 | Rogers Arena

10 Rogers Arena, Vancouver

ʻe fans are still waiting for a Stanley Cup, but in 2010 it was the setting of the Olympic
ʻl final between Canada and the U.S., one of the best international games in the

No. 1 | Bell Centre

9. MTS Centre, Winnipeg

Yeah, it's small and missing the original Queen's photo from the since-demolished Winnipeg Arena, but after losing their team once already, there might not be a more appreciative fan base in the entire NHL.

8. Bridgestone Arena, Nashville

With country singer Carrie Underwood cheering on Mike Fisher in the luxury suites and a thriving bar scene just steps outside, it's no wonder hockey has found a foothold in Nashville.

7. Consol Energy Center, Pittsburgh

The Pens' old home, Mellon Arena – previously the Civic Arena or 'The Igloo' –was the setting for the Jean-Claude Van Damme movie *Sudden Death*, but the 'House That Sidney Built' is the first Leadership in Energy and Environmental Design (LEED) gold-certified arena in North America.

6. Air Canada Centre, Toronto

The banners celebrating championship after championship are an ever-looming reminder for fans who have not seen the Stanley Cup since 1967, but they're proof the Leafs were once a successful team. Seriously. Followers of the Blue and White won't likely see that drought snapped soon, but at least they can enjoy mediocre hockey in world-class surroundings.

5. Joe Louis Arena, Detroit

Sure, 'The Joe' might be in need of some TLC, but in terms of traditions there is nothing better watching a fan charging down the stairs and launching an octopus onto the ice to get things started.

4. Wells Fargo Center, Philadelphia

Word of advice: do not wear an opposing jersey to a Flyers game. The rabid fans here care about their team and sure like to make it known.

3. United Center, Chicago

Whether it is the roar of the crowd during the national anthem or hearing *Chelsea Dagger* by the Fratellis after a goal is scored, Chicago has created an environment that other cities can only dream of.

2. Madison Square Garden, New York

Give the Rangers credit for their recent renovations to the original arena, which include a see-through wall so fans can now watch players walk to the rink from the dressing room.

1. ` Centre, Montreal

ot nearly as much history as the old Forum, but Montreal is still the No. 1 place to stly because of the fans. The hot dogs help, too. ▨

PLAYOFF COMEBACKS

The regular season is just an extended prelude to the most exciting time of year – the playoffs. Each series is epic in its own right, from merciless sweeps to back-and-forth exchanges decided by a single goal in Game 7. But there's something very special about a team climbing out from an early hole to beat the odds to move on.

Only 21 times has a team come back after falling behind 3-1 in a series and only thrice has a team managed to win after going down 3-0. Not surprisingly, that trio makes up this list's top three, with 3-1 series deficits accounting for the first seven. – LB

No. 3 | Philadelphia vs. Boston

10. Montreal vs. Boston – 2004, Round 1

The Canadiens were the No. 7 seed and the Bruins No. 2 in this opening-round tilt. Richard Zednik scored both goals in a 2-0 Game 7 win. Unfortunately for the Habs, they were swept by eventual Stanley Cup champ Tampa Bay in the following round.

9. New Jersey vs. Philadelphia – 2000, Round 3

This comeback is overshadowed by the defining moment of the 2000 playoffs: the massive hit Devils defenseman Scott Stevens laid on Flyers star Eric Lindros. The Devils moved on to beat the Dallas Stars on Jason Arnott's Game 6 double overtime-winner to win the Cup. Lindros never played another game for the Flyers.

8. Minnesota vs. Vancouver – 2003, Round 2

The 2003 playoffs were filled with Game 7s, six of them to be exact. The biggest of the bunch came when the Wild topped the Canucks to complete their second 3-1 series comeback of the playoffs. To top it off, they fell behind 2-0 in Game 7 before rallying for a 4-2 win. Minny's luck ran out there, however. They were stomped 4-0 by the Ducks in the next round.

7. Vancouver vs. Calgary – 1994, Round 1

A trio of Canucks took it upon themselves to drive Vancouver to an upset victory. Geoff Courtnall, Trevor Linden and Pavel Bure scored three straight overtime game-winning goals to move the Canucks into the second round and eventually a Stanley Cup final date with the New York Rangers.

6. Edmonton vs. Winnipeg – 1990, Round 1

Led by Mark Messier and Bill Ranford, the star-powered Edmonton squad charged back, defeating Winnipeg en route to their fifth Stanley Cup victory in seven years.

5. Washington vs. Philadelphia – 1988, Round 1

With 56 goals scored over the seven games of this series, it was the highest scoring playoff matchup in 1988. With 'Iron' Mike Keenan at the helm, the Flyers took a commanding lead over Bryan Murray's Capitals. Alas, Washington would force a Game 7 and in overtime Caps legend Dale Hunter would put the series-winning goal past 1987 Vezina Trophy-winner Ron Hextall to complete the comeback.

4. New York vs. Washington – 1987, Round 1

Capped off by the Game 7 'Easter Epic' masterpiece, the 1987 Patrick Division semifinal was a series for the ages. Carried by the unbelievable performance of netminder Kelly Hrudey (73 saves), New York outlasted the Caps as Pat LaFontaine scored at 8:47 of the fourth overtime period to complete the comeback.

3. Philadelphia vs. Boston – 2010, Round 2

The Flyers and Bruins were meeting for the first time in the playoffs since 1978 and early on it didn't appear it would be much of a contest. However, losing No. 1 center David Krejci to a broken wrist in the Game 3 win proved costly for Boston, as the Flyers would fight back with four straight victories. The icing on the cake was a Game 7 win that saw the Flyers overcome a first period 3-0 deficit.

2. New York vs. Pittsburgh – 1975, Round 1

A half-decade before the 1980s Isles dynasty emerged, the franchise etched its name in the   ory books in this 1975 series with the Pittsburgh Penguins. New York erased the 3-0   cit before 'Chico' Resch sealed the turnaround with a Game 7, 1-0 shutout win. J.P   's father – potted the only goal of the game 11 seconds into overtime.

1. Toronto vs. Detroit – 1942, Stanley Cup final

Toronto opened the 1942 Stanley Cup final in disastrous fashion, losing three straight games, including two at home. Leafs coach Hap Day was so infuriated he benched his regulars, placing Toronto's hopes in the hands of a group of upstart rookies. The move worked. With veteran tender Turk Broda playing at the top of his game, the Leafs became the first and only team to ever erase a 3-0 series deficit to win the Stanley Cup. THN

No. 1 | Toronto vs. Detroit

ROOKIE GOALIES

The list of Calder Trophy winners is almost entirely comprised of forwards and D-men. Only 16 goalies have been given the honor since it was first awarded in 1937. That speaks to how infrequently a rookie keeper makes a significant impact with his club.

   Here are the best of the few goalies who've rocked the socks off of the NHL in their freshman campaign. **- JG & TR**

No. 9 | Ken Dryden

10. Glenn Resch, Islanders 1975-76

   If not for a mind-blowing performance by teammate Bryan Trottier (32 goals, 95 points), 'Chico' likely would have won the Calder Trophy in 1976. Resch finished second in the league with an astounding goals-against average of 2.07, second in shutouts (seven) and was top 10 in wins despite the fact that he was splitting time in net with the fiery Billy Smith. The native of Moose Jaw, Sask., received second team all-star honors.

9. Ken Dryden, Montreal, 1971-72

Ken Dryden took over the Montreal Canadiens crease during the playoffs in 1971 and proved to be a towering pillar of strength. Dryden won the Conn Smythe Trophy as the Habs collected their 17th Cup. In his following rookie season, the 6-foot-4 Dryden continued his stellar play, leading the league in wins (39) while placing fourth in GAA (2.24) and second in shutouts (eight). He was named to the second all-star team and won the Calder Trophy.

8. Glenn Hall, Detroit, 1955-56

Detroit GM Jack Adams had so much confidence in what Glenn Hall had displayed during a two-game call-up in 1954-55 that he dealt the Vezina-winning Terry Sawchuk to the Boston Bruins prior to the 1955-56 season. Adams' risk quickly turned to reward as Hall played all 70 games for the Red Wings, finishing second to Jacques Plante in GAA (2.10), third in wins (30) and first in shutouts (12). He was named a second team all-star and awarded the Calder Trophy.

7. Roger Crozier, Detroit, 1964-65

It isn't every season that a rookie is given the opportunity to usurp the throne from one of the games greats. But that is exactly what happened in 1964-65 when Roger Crozier showed up on the scene in Detroit. Crozier played every game for the Wings (70) and led the league in wins (40) and shutouts (six). He finished second in GAA (2.42), was awarded the Calder Trophy and a place on the first all-star team. His performance was so remarkable that Detroit placed future Hall-of-Famer Terry Sawchuk on waivers.

6. Ron Hextall, Philadelphia, 1986-87

Ron Hextall stormed through the league during his 13-year NHL career and his rookie season was no exception. Leading the league in games played (66), wins (37) and save percentage (.902), Hextall carried the Flyers to a second-place regular season finish and an appearance in the Cup final. Despite losing to the powerhouse Oilers, Hextall was awarded the Conn Smythe Trophy. He also grabbed the Vezina Trophy and a spot on the first all-star team.

5. Bill Durnan, Montreal, 1943-44

Over the course of a seven-year NHL career, Durnan won the Vezina Trophy an astonishing six times, including his rookie season in 1943-44. Durnan earned every bit of that award as he was the only goalie to play every minute of every game that season. His league-leading goals-against average (2.18) was .82 better than the runner-up and he had 21 more wins (38) than any other goalie that season. Durnan led the Habs to a Stanley Cup victory and was recognized with a place on the first all-star team.

4. Terry Sawchuk, Detroit, 1950-51

Sawchuk entered the NHL as the starting goalie for the defending Cup-champion Wings and played every minute of every game, compiling a 44-13-13 record. Sawchuk led the league in shutouts with 11, finished second with a 1.99 GAA and first in victories. He was named a first team all-star and rookie of the year. He missed out on the Vezina Trophy – originally awarded to the goalie allowing the fewest goals against – by a single goal.

3. Tom Barrasso, Buffalo, 1983-84

Barrasso entered the NHL right out of high school as an 18-year-old and supplanted Bob Sauve as Buffalo's No. 1 netminder. In 42 games he went 26-12-3 with two shutouts, a 2.84 GAA and an .893 save percentage. That may not seem like a great stat line, but this was the offense-driven NHL of the early 1980s – Wayne Gretzky tallied 205 points that season. Barrasso's GAA was second in the league, his save percentage third. He was named to the all-rookie and first all-star teams and won the Calder and Vezina trophies.

2. Ed Belfour, Chicago, 1990-91

Belfour didn't pick up the moniker 'Eddie the Eagle' until later in his career, but he was certainly a high flyer during his rookie season. Belfour saw action in 74 games, compiling a 43-19-7 record with four shutouts, a league-leading .910 save percentage and a 2.47 GAA. He won the Jennings, Calder and Vezina Trophies, and was named to the NHL's first all-star team and the all-rookie team.

1. Tony Esposito, Chicago, 1969-70

What is it about Chicago rookie puck stoppers? Tony 'O' not only had the best rookie goaltender season the NHL has ever seen, he may have had the best rookie season in NHL history, period. Esposito went 38-17-8 to lead the league in victories, finished with a 2.17 GAA and set a modern record that still stands with 15 shutouts. For his efforts, he won the Calder and Vezina Trophies and was named a first team all-star.

No. 1 | Tony Esposito

LONGEST GAMES

There must be some sort of value in winning a marathon playoff game: nine out of 10 teams to win one of these lengthy matches went on to be victorious in the series.

Perhaps the momentum earned from such a win is critical to a team's playoff success while the momentum lost can be a deathblow? Whatever the case, these are the longest games in NHL history. **– Michael Stephens**

10. New York Islanders 3, Washington Capitals 2 – 1987 (8:47 4OT)
The 'Easter Epic' began on a Saturday and ended early Easter Sunday morning. Originally trailing in the series 3-1, the Isles fought back, with Pat LaFontaine, then a playoff underachiever, getting the monkey off his back by potting the series-clinching goal on a shot from the point.

9. Montreal Canadiens 2, New York Rangers 1 – 1930 (8:52 4OT)
In the first game of the 1930 Stanley Cup semifinal, injury call-up Gus Rivers broke the stalemate with his only point of the playoffs. *Les Habitants* went on to sweep the Rangers and then the Bruins to take Lord Stanley's mug.

8. Dallas Stars 2, San Jose Sharks 1 – 2008 (9:03 of 4OT)
Brenden Morrow played the hero and Marty Turco (the losing goalie of record in a couple other games on this list) received some measure of overtime redemption in Game 1 of the Western Conference semifinal.

7. Toronto Maple Leafs 3, Detroit Red Wings 2 – 1943 (10:18 of 4OT)
Jack McLean scored for the road team halfway through the fourth overtime, though his Leafs eventually lost in the semifinal in six games. As an engineering student at the University of Toronto, McLean was typically barred from travel to the United States as a wartime precaution. He was allowed across the border during certain times of the year, including this playoff series with the Wings.

6. Vancouver Canucks 5, Dallas Stars 4 – 2007 (18:06 of 4OT)
Henrik Sedin's marker was a typical twin play, with Daniel corralling the puck behind the Stars net and finding his brother sifting through the slot to victimize Turco.

5. Pittsburgh Penguins 3, Washington Capitals 2 – 1996 (19:15 of 4OT)
The 1996 Penguins had three of the top-10 scorers of all-time (Mario Lemieux, Jaromir Jagr and Ron Francis) and yet it was defector Petr Nedved who stole the spotlight. The longest game in 60 years was ended by the Czech ex-pat, who slapped the puck past Olaf Kolzig in the Eastern Conference quarterfinal.

No. 3 | Philadelphia vs. Pittsburgh

4. Anaheim Ducks 4, Dallas Stars 3 – 2003 (0:48 of 5OT)

Regular season and playoffs combined, Petr Sykora scored 38 goals in Anaheim in 2002-03. None was more important than the winner in Game 1 of the West semifinal. Just 48 seconds into the fifth OT period, Adam Oates flipped a centering pass to Sykora who one-timed the puck past poor ol' Turco.

3. Philadelphia Flyers 2, Pittsburgh Penguins 1 – 2000 (12:01 of 5OT)

Much maligned for his playoff shortcomings, Keith Primeau silenced critics with a nifty flick of the wrists. Primeau entered the zone along the right wing before cutting in around Darius Kasparaitis and rifling a shot short side under the crossbar on Ron Tugnutt, who made 70 saves in the loss.

2. Toronto Maple Leafs 1, Boston Bruins 0 – 1933 (4:06 of 6OT)

Diminutive journeyman Ken Doraty helped the 'Gashouse Gang' punch their ticket to the Cup final by scoring in the sixth overtime period. 'Cagie' Ken also netted one of the most puzzling feats in hockey history: he once tallied a natural hat trick *in overtime* in 1934 (prior to the adoption of the sudden-death format) leading the Buds to a 7-4 victory over the Ottawa Senators.

1. Detroit 1, Montreal Maroons 0 – 1936 (16:30 of 6OT)

In the 1936 Stanley Cup semifinal, Modere 'Mud' Bruneteau broke a 0-0 scoreless tie just prior to the completion of the ninth period of play. The rookie call-up slid the puck past reigning Vezina Trophy winner Lorne Chabot for the win. Poor 'Chabotsky' was probably still trying to catch his breath after playing for the Leafs in the second-longest overtime game (see No. 2). THN

MOST GAMES PLAYED
WITH ONE TEAM

Lost in the shuffle of Nicklas Lidstrom's four Stanley Cups, seven Norris Trophies, one Conn Smythe and a dozen all-star team berths is an achievement once thought unattainable. Late in 2011-12, Lidstrom passed fellow Red Wings great Alex Delvecchio for most games played with one franchise.

It's a feat that took 20 years to reach during an era when it would have been so easy to forego. The lowering age of free agency, the growing number of teams and the temptation to hit the jackpot as an unrestricted free agent once made Delvecchio's standard unreachable – presumably.

*Delvecchio spent his entire career with one organization, from 1951 to 1974. Only nine other players in the history of the game had played that many regular season contests with one organization until Lidstrom matched and passed him. Like Delvecchio – and the No. 3 on our list – things just worked out well in Detroit. There was never any reason to leave. These are the leaders in games played with one organization. – **BC***

10. Gilbert Perreault, Buffalo, 1,191

Perreault and the 'French Connection' line made Buffalo a bilingual city for 17 seasons. Besides making the grade on this roll, he finds him among elite company on some other lists, too: he's top 40 all-time in goals, game-winners and points.

9. Martin Brodeur, New Jersey 1,191

Brodeur is the only goaltender among the top 10 and is at nearly twice the games of the next most loyal goalie of all-time (Toronto's Turk Broda, 629 games). We'll give him the nod over Perreault as Brodeur, despite losing to Los Angeles in the 2012 Cup final, wasn't done stopping pucks for the Devils just yet.

8. Shane Doan, Phoenix/Winnipeg, 1,198

The seventh overall draft pick by the Jets in 1995 played one season as a teenager in Winnipeg before the franchise moved to Phoenix in 1996. The Alberta native is well known for his love of the western lifestyle and has established a horse ranch in Arizona.

7. Henri Richard, Montreal, 1,256

Rocket Richard's little brother had a quick trigger himself and a fabulous sense of timing: he has an NHL-high 11 Stanley Cup rings. 'The Pocket Rocket' retired in 1975 at age 39. Had he been fit and willing enough to play another four seasons, he would have 15 Cup rings as Montreal won four straight after he retired.

No. 10 | Gilbert Perreault

6. Ken Daneyko, New Jersey, 1,283

New Jersey's great Scotts – Stevens and Niedermayer – got a lot more points and headlines than Daneyko, but the stay-at-home rearguard was a crucial cog in three Stanley Cup victories. He retired a Cup champion at 39 in 2003 having played 175 career playoff games with the Devils.

5. Joe Sakic, Colorado/Quebec, 1,378

Sakic spent his first seven seasons playing with a young and struggling franchise in Quebec before the team moved to Colorado and immediately won a Stanley Cup. He played another 13 seasons with the Avalanche and was regarded as the most respected player in the game during the twilight of his career.

4. Stan Mikita, Chicago, 1,394

Mikita was a feisty playmaking center during the Hawks' glory years in the early 1960s, averaging more than 100 PIM his first six seasons before transforming his temper and going on to win a pair of Lady Byng Trophies with 12 and 14 PIM seasons.

3. Steve Yzerman, Detroit, 1,514

The quintessential leader of the Red Wings was a high-flying offensive kingpin during the early part of his career and a two-way leader later on, guiding Detroit to three Stanley Cup titles in a six-year window.

2. Alex Delvecchio, Detroit, 1,549

Delvecchio played in the shadow of Gordie Howe for most of his 23 full seasons with the Red Wings, but in his own right was a crafty, productive producer, topping out at 83 points as a 36-year old in 1968-69. He won Cups three of his first four seasons in the league, but none after that.

1. Nicklas Lidstrom, Detroit, 1,564

Yzerman and Lidstrom were teammates for 1,096 games (the last of Yzerman's streak and the first of Lidstrom's streak) and there were few more durable in the game than the Swedish defenseman. He missed just 44 games in 21 NHL seasons, 12 of them coming in 2011-12, his last campaign. THN

No. 1 | Nicklas Lidstrom

10	ELSA/GETTY IMAGES
15	DENIS BRODEUR/NHLI VIA GETTY IMAGES
17	S. LEVY/BRUCE BENNETT STUDIOS/GETTY IMAGES
19	JUKKA RAUTIO/GETTY IMAGES
20	ROBERT LABERGE/ALL SPORT
22	ANDY DEVLIN/NHLI VIA GETTY IMAGES
23	MIKE STOBE/NHLI VIA GETTY IMAGES
25	G FIUME/GETTY IMAGES
26	CLAUS ANDERSEN/GETTY IMAGES
27	FREDERICK BREEDON/GETTY IMAGES
30	COURTESY AIR FORCE ACADEMY
31	COURTESY ALASKA ACES
33	BRAD WATSON/NHLI VIA GETTY IMAGES
35	BRUCE BENNETT STUDIOS/GETTY IMAGES
36	MARCO CAMPANELLI/GETTY IMAGES
38	ROBERT LABERGE/ALL SPORT
39	JOHN GIAMUNDO/GETTY IMAGES
40	BRUCE BENNETT/GETTY IMAGES
43	DOUG PENSINGER/GETTY IMAGES
45	BILL SMITH/NHLI VIA GETTY IMAGES
47	MECHIOR DIGIACOMO/GETTY IMAGES
48	STAFF/AFP/GETTY IMAGES
49	B BENNETT/GETTY IMAGES
51	BRUCE BENNETT STUDIOS/GETTY IMAGES
53	DENIS BRODEUR/NHLI VIA GETTY IMAGES
56	BRUCE BENNETT STUDIOS/GETTY IMAGES
59	DAVE SANDFORD/GETTY IMAGES
61	BRUCE BENNETT STUDIOS/GETTY IMAGES
62	SCOTT AUDETTE/NHLI VIA GETTY IMAGES
64	BRUCE BENNETT STUDIOS/GETTY IMAGES
65	BRUCE BENNETT STUDIOS/GETTY IMAGES
67	BRUCE BENNETT STUDIOS/GETTY IMAGES
69	BRUCE BENNETT STUDIOS/GETTY IMAGES
71	BRUCE BENNETT STUDIOS/GETTY IMAGES
75	JOHN RUSSELL/NHLI VIA GETTY IMAGES
78	FOCUS ON SPORT/GETTY IMAGES
81	ALL SPORT/ALL SPORT
83	BRUCE BENNETT STUDIOS/GETTY IMAGES
84	BRUCE BENNETT STUDIOS/GETTY IMAGES
87	DENIS BRODEUR/NHLI VIA GETTY IMAGES
88	JIM MCISAAC/GETTY IMAGES
90	TODD WARSHAW/POOL/GETTY IMAGES
91	CHARLES HOFF/NY DAILY NEWS VIA GETTY IMAGES
93	STEVE BABINEAU/NHLI VIA GETTY IMAGES
95	BRUCE BENNETT STUDIOS/GETTY IMAGES
96	BRUCE BENNETT STUDIOS/GETTY IMAGES
97	ANDY DEVLIN/NHLI VIA GETTY IMAGES
99	GRAIG ABEL/NHLI VIA GETTY IMAGES
100	B BENNETT/GETTY IMAGES
104	BRUCE BENNETT STUDIOS/GETTY IMAGES
107	B BENNETT/GETTY IMAGES
108	PICTORIAL PARADE/GETTY IMAGES
112	MECHIOR DIGIACOMO/GETTY IMAGES
113	MECHIOR DIGIACOMO/GETTY IMAGES
115	DAVE REGINEK/NHLI VIA GETTY IMAGES
117	DENIS BRODEUR/ NHLI VIA GETTY IMAGES
118	BRUCE BENNETT STUDIOS/GETTY IMAGES
121	BRUCE BENNETT STUDIOS/GETTY IMAGES
122	DON SMITH/NHLI VIA GETTY IMAGES

123	STEVE BABINEAU/NHLI VIA GETTY IMAGES
125	BRIAN BAHR/GETTY IMAGES
126	BRUCE BENNETT/GETTY IMAGES
129	DENIS BRODEUR/ NHLI VIA GETTY IMAGES
131	B BENNETT/GETTY IMAGES
132	PHILLIP MACCALLUM/GETTY IMAGES
135	GREGORY SHAMUS/GETTY IMAGES
137	DENIS BRODEUR/ NHLI VIA GETTY IMAGES
138	GREGORY SHAMUS/NHLI VIA GETTY IMAGES
139	BRUCE BENNETT STUDIOS/GETTY IMAGES
141	DENIS BRODEUR/ NHLI VIA GETTY IMAGES
143	B BENNETT/GETTY IMAGES
144	GREGG FORWERCK/NHLI VIA GETTY IMAGES
145	GREGG FORWERCK/NHLI VIA GETTY IMAGES
149	BRUCE BENNETT STUDIOS/GETTY IMAGES
150	BRUCE BENNETT STUDIOS/GETTY IMAGES
151	BRUCE BENNETT STUDIOS/GETTY IMAGES
153	DENIS BRODEUR/ NHLI VIA GETTY IMAGES
155	DAVE SANDFORD/GETTY IMAGES
157	BRUCE BENNETT STUDIOS/GETTY IMAGES
161	BRUCE BENNETT STUDIOS/GETTY IMAGEST
163	BRUCE BENNETT STUDIOS/GETTY IMAGES
166	DENIS BRODEUR/ NHLI VIA GETTY IMAGES
167	BRUCE BENNETT STUDIOS/GETTY IMAGES
168	B BENNETT/GETTY IMAGES
170	BRUCE BENNETT STUDIOS/GETTY IMAGES
173	ANDY MARLIN/NHLI VIA GETTY IMAGES
175	XXXXXXXXX SLAP SHOT
177	DILIP VISHWANAT/SPORTING NEWS/ICON SMI
179	FOCUS ON SPORT/GETTY IMAGES
180	MECHIOR DIGIACOMO/GETTY IMAGES
182	HARRY HOW/GETTY IMAGES
184	MECHIOR DIGIACOMO/GETTY IMAGES
185	HULTON ARCHIVE/GETTY IMAGES
187	BRUCE BENNETT STUDIOS/GETTY IMAGES
188	BRUCE BENNETT STUDIOS/GETTY IMAGES
190	BRUCE BENNETT STUDIOS/GETTY IMAGES
192	BRUCE BENNETT STUDIOS/GETTY IMAGES
193	BRUCE BENNETT STUDIOS/GETTY IMAGES
195	GRAIG ABEL/NHLI VIA GETTY IMAGES
197	SCOTT LEVY/GETTY IMAGES
198	BRUCE BENNETT STUDIOS/GETTY IMAGES
200	DAVE SANDFORD/NHLI VIA GETTY IMAGES
202	JONATHAN DANIEL/GETTY IMAGES
205	GREGORY SHAMUS/NHLI VIA GETTY IMAGES
207	BRUCE BENNETT STUDIOS/GETTY IMAGES
208	JEFF VINNICK/NHLI VIA GETTY IMAGES
210	SCOTT CUNNINGHAM/NHLI VIA GETTY IMAGES
211	ELSA/ALL SPORT
213	KEITH TORRIE/NY DAILY NEWS ARCHIVE VIA GETTY IMAGES
214	DEREK LEUNG/GETTY IMAGES
215	FRANCOIS LACASSE/NHLI VIA GETTY IMAGES
217	BRIAN BABINEAU/NHLI VIA GETTY IMAGES
219	BRUCE BENNETT STUDIOS/GETTY IMAGES
220	DENIS BRODEUR/ NHLI VIA GETTY IMAGES
223	BRUCE BENNETT STUDIOS/GETTY IMAGES
225	DOUG PENSINGER/ALL SPORT
227	MECHIOR DIGIACOMO/GETTY IMAGES
229	GRAIG ABEL/NHLI VIA GETTY IMAGES

ACKNOWLEDGMENTS

THANKS GO OUT TO EVERYONE INVOLVED IN THE PROJECT, WITH A SPECIAL TIP OF THE CAP TO:

- THN editor in chief, Jason Kay, for his standard ever-steady wise guidance.

- The editorial staff – Rory Boylen, Ken Campbell, Ryan Kennedy, Matt Larkin, Adam Proteau and Ronnie Shuker – and the interns – Jason Chen, Casey Ippolito, Brian Liu, Bryan Mcwilliam, Andrew Mendler, Kyle Palantzas, Michael Stephens and, especially, Liz Bevan and Taylor Rocca – for their work in writing, editing and fact-checking.

- Former THN family member John Grigg and contributors Bob Duff, Denis Gibbons and Michael Traikos for their knowledge and creativity.

- THN art director Erika Vanderveer for her work on the cover, photo research and layout and Diane Marquette for her assistance.

- Tracy Finkelstein, Carlie McGhee and Erin Quinn in the marketing/communications department for helping get the word out.

- And the management duo of THN publisher Caroline Andrews and book publisher Jean Pare for their work behind the scenes.